Spirituality for Lent and Easter

A Guide for Bridging the Mysteries

by
Gerard F. Baumbach

PAULIST PRESS
New York/Mahwah, New Jersey

The Publisher gratefully acknowledges use of the following: Excerpts from the *New American Bible* Copyright © 1991, 1986, 1970, Confraternity of Christian Doctrine, Inc. Washington, D.C. Reprinted with permission. All rights reserved. Excerpts from the *Lectionary for Mass for Use in the Dioceses of the United States, second typical edition* Copyright © 1998, 1997, 1970, Confraternity of Christian Doctrine, Inc., Washington, D.C. Reprinted with permission. All rights reserved. Excerpt from the English translation of the *Catechism of the Catholic Church* for the United States of America © 1994, United States Catholic Conference, Inc.—Libreria Editrice Vaticana. Used with permission. Excerpt from the English translation of *Rite of Christian Initiation of Adults* © 1985, International Committee on English in the Liturgy, Inc. All rights reserved. Excerpt from *St. John Chrysostom: Baptismal Instructions,* translated and annotated by P.W. Harkins (Ancient Christian Writers, Vol. 31), published by Newman Press, New York, copyright 1963 by Rev. Johannes Quasten and Rev. Walter J. Burghardt, S.J. Excerpt from *St. Ambrose: Theological and Dogmatic Works,* translated by R.J. Deferrari (Fathers of the Church, Vol. 44), copyright 1963, The Catholic University of America Press. The poem "Baptism" by Elaine Holena-Baumbach, 1978. Used with permission.

Interior art by Emil Antonucci

Cover design by Nicholas T. Markell

Book design by Theresa M. Sparacio

Copyright © 1998 by Gerard F. Baumbach

Library of Congress Cataloging-in-Publication Data

Baumbach, Gerard F.
   Spirituality for Lent and Easter : a guide for bridging the mysteries / by Gerard F. Baumbach.
     p. cm.
     ISBN 0-8091-3837-9 (alk. paper)
   1. Lent—Prayer-books and devotions—English. 2. Holy Week—Prayer-books and devotions—English. 3. Eastertide—Prayer-books and devotions—English. 4. Catholic Church—Prayer-books and devotions—English. 5. Bible—Liturgical lessons, English. I. Title.
BX2170.L4B38   1998
242'.34—dc21   98-34868
                                                 CIP

Published by Paulist Press
997 Macarthur Boulevard
Mahwah, New Jersey 07430

www.paulistpress.com

Printed and bound in the United States of America

CONTENTS

To my wife
Elaine
reflection of the mystery of life and
reminder to me of the wisdom of the eternal God

ACKNOWLEDGMENTS

This book is, in some ways, the result of many conversations on Christian spirituality. Indeed, I am indebted to many people who helped me in one way or another during the writing of this book. I would be remiss, however, if I did not thank Dr. Norman F. Josaitis for his precise insights and wise counsel as he reviewed the manuscript. This friend and colleague often provided a twist of a phrase and an alternative way of viewing a topic that opened new doors to me in exploring chapter themes. I am grateful for his kind assistance in the review of the book.

Paulist Press once again enabled me to work with Maria L. Maggi, editor of both this and my prior book. Her work on the manuscript, availability for consultation and kind and gracious way of moving the project along bear testimony to the expertise she brings to her publisher and to the industry in which we both serve. However, the responsibility for what appears here remains my own.

INTRODUCTION

The seasons of Lent and Easter flow from a single river of faith lived and life transformed. These seasons converge around the three most sacred days of the year, the sacred triduum that bridges Holy Thursday—Good Friday—Holy Saturday—and Easter Sunday.

There is no escaping our immersion into the mysteries of the seasons. Our weekly worship and daily time set aside for prayer, our actions on behalf of the gospel and our heightened awareness of Christ present in others enable us to enter the depths of Christian mystery in new and surprising ways.

We find new meanings in the flowing waters of baptism, the saturation with the oil of confirmation and the sharing of the sacred meal of the eucharist. We witness by prayer, alms-giving and fasting the mercy, love, justice and wonder of almighty God in our relationships with others.

Why, then, this book?

Spirituality for Lent and Easter: A Guide for Bridging the Mysteries is written to support your growing awareness of what it is to live the Christian life during the time of Lent and Easter. The book can help you to bridge the mysteries as you focus first on the Lenten Sundays and conclude with meditation on the Sundays of the Easter season. The link, or bridge, joining the two seasons together is the Easter triduum, that most holy time of the church year in which we recall and enter into with a new and Spirit-driven dynamism the mystery of God-with-us in Jesus Christ.

We will renew the promises of baptism at Easter. We will join with the newly baptized and those received into the church at the eucharistic table. Before this, however, we will have walked with them for weeks, months and perhaps years, ensuring that they experience firsthand the faith and care of their brothers and sisters. All of us are part of the faith community that celebrates the mysteries of life during these seasons.

This book offers an opportunity to link your life more concretely to the lives of all who are coming to faith—those approaching the sacraments for the first time as well as parishioners you may have known for many years.

Each chapter of the book focuses on a Sunday of the Lenten season or Easter season, or the Easter triduum. The Lenten Sunday readings, from Cycle A of the church's three-year cycle of readings, offer particularly important insights for us as we pray with and for those coming to the Easter sacraments. Similarly, readings from the same cycle for the Easter season form a springboard for faith growth and reflection for the community of believers as we emerge from the celebration of the Easter triduum.

Each chapter includes four basic parts to guide your reflection: *Exploring Your Experience, Exploring the Scriptures, Renewing Your Life of Faith* and *Accepting the Challenge.* These four parts, taken together, are simply one way of entering into the mystery of each of the Sundays. The theme of each chapter is drawn from the scriptures of that Sunday. You are invited to explore the theme as you find it surfacing in *your* life. You can also consider ways of renewing the gift of faith, perhaps determining as well some new and practical ways of accepting the challenge of living a life of faith.

You can read at your own pace, moving through a chapter in a single meditation, or more gradually, according to the chapter parts just named. The questions that usually appear at the end of a section can be used to aid your reflection and meditation.

You might find it helpful to participate with other people from your parish, sharing reflections and exploring the scriptures with them.

Our life of discipleship in Christ is a common life, a life of community lived in relationship with others. What is right about our relationships? What challenges us? What might we need to change? Our walk through the mysteries helps us to explore such questions. We gather for prayer and worship together, support one another in our daily living of the gospel and seek the justice of God as a people united in the Holy Spirit.

Do not be shy about inviting another parishioner to walk with you during these Lenten-Easter days! Remember especially those who are preparing for the Easter sacraments, people who have been walking in faith under the supportive arms of your parish. They need your ongoing prayer, welcome and example of Christian discipleship.

It is my hope that *Spirituality for Lent and Easter: A Guide for Bridging the Mysteries* will be helpful as you walk in faith during the coming weeks. May it enrich your meditation and reflection and motivate you to pray with others, as together you enter the mysteries of the faith you treasure and proclaim.

A Closing Thought

The approach for dealing with the themes of this book was influenced by a book I wrote for newly baptized Catholics called *Experiencing Mystagogy: The Sacred Pause of Easter* (Paulist Press, 1996). That book enables newly baptized adults to explore the mysteries of faith they have just experienced in the Easter sacraments of baptism, confirmation and eucharist.

What led to the publication of *Spirituality for Lent and Easter: A Guide for Bridging the Mysteries* were the requests of people of faith to make available to *all* adult parishioners an approach similar to that provided for the newly baptized. Reflection on the mysteries of faith, after all, is the business of all of us, and there is no better time to renew our faith than the Lenten and Easter seasons.

CHAPTER 1:
BREATH OF LIFE, GRACIOUS GIFT

First Sunday of Lent

Exploring Your Experience

The first Sunday of Lent offers a look at God's creative initiative through the biblical story of the birth of humanity. The Lord God not only forms the first living beings, but breathes into his creation the breath of life.

As you begin your spiritual journey bridging Lent and Easter, consider what or who it is that helps to give life to your faith. Immerse yourself in the quiet time of these next ninety days in a rediscovery of the *breath of life* that permeates every fiber of your being. Such a suggestion may be contrary to what we are "supposed to do" to prepare for Easter and the days that follow—make time to shop for that new outfit, ensure that we find the right basket of candy or fruit, get ready for springtime and so on.

Each year during Lent the church reminds us of the majesty and wonder of the gracious gift of God's creation. We become new again, or "re-newed," as we ponder the mysteries that lie at the core of our faith. We fast, we pray, we do good works—all ways of asserting a spirit of penance and conversion to Christ.

We journey in faith, in life and in spirit, not alone but with other believers—regular people just like us whose own commitment to living in the creative embrace of God finds central

5

place in their lives, too. Along the way, we build bridges together, in our families, our parishes, our workplaces. We become a people bonded together in a common purpose of union with one another in Jesus Christ.

- *Who helps you to breathe the breath of faith, the breath of life? When have you been renewed by another person? Was this a blessed experience for you?*
- *How do you affirm other people's commitment to live their faith? Can you be a bridge of renewal and hope for a friend or stranger? How?*

Exploring the Scriptures

The readings for the first Sunday of Lent are:

- *Genesis 2:7–9; 3:1–7*
- *Romans 5:12–19*
- *Matthew 4:1–11*

The readings for this Sunday are rich in images that are as relevant to us today as they were when first written, under the inspiration of the Holy Spirit, thousands of years ago. Select one or more of the readings for your reflection. The following ideas may help you to choose or lead you in new directions.

Genesis 2:7–9; 3:1–7

The first joint in your Lenten-Easter bridge comes from the first breath that enlivens humankind. This is the breath of the Holy Spirit, a breath that moves as the wind among people and that moves people to enliven others by their Christian discipleship.

But what if such breath is cut off? How are we to respond to a cunning snatcher of life? Such a dilemma is presented to us in the image of the serpent—that misleading evil One who seeks not life, but death, who desires to rule all people with sinister madness and who demands compliance. In the sin of Adam and Eve, we see the powerful (but not *all*-powerful) grasp of the tempter of those who would otherwise seek good.

How might we ensure that we remain strong against challenges to what we believe? How are we called to live? Begin by considering the following:

- *What or who is your "tempter"?*
- *How might you breathe life into a relationship in your family, community or parish?*

Romans 5:12–19

We are reminded here of Adam, "the type of the one who was to come." That one to come is, of course, Jesus Christ. Jesus of Nazareth comes in the simplest yet most sacred of ways—through human birth. Through the gift of this one, all are offered the gift of new life, so "the many will be made righteous." Through him, all are made new in the offer of grace of the God who calls and who comes, who breathes and who moves among all creation. How wonderful the mighty God!

The incarnation—the mystery of the Word becoming flesh—is only the beginning of these specially graced moments of humanity. Jesus, gift of our gracious God, goes on to give his all for all, gifting us with the wonder of new life through his humble yet fervent obedience. The cross is that symbol of suffering and triumph that states without words what we have known for two millennia. The cross is symbol of salvation to us, that bridge to eternity. We need to look upon the cross again and again.

Jesus' death yields life, his resurrection the enlivening presence of the breath of the Holy Spirit in our midst.

This Lent, focus on Jesus Christ in new ways. What does his suffering—his complete giving of self all life long—suggest to you about the suffering of others or yourself today? About the giving of yourself or your parish? How might you find in Jesus support for burdens you carry or assist others to carry?

• *Meditate during this week on the obedience of the One who would not only proclaim justice but also make it victorious (see Matthew 12:18–21 and Isaiah 42:1–4). Ask yourself how, by living justly, you might be renewed as a child of the just God. Where might you begin? What threshold might you have to cross to make this happen?*

Matthew 4:1–11

We return to the tempter. Perhaps you thought the first reading would exhaust the evil One. Somehow Satan might be satisfied, knowing that the cunning nature of the prince of darkness could affect all humanity. Be done with it, Satan!

Our focus here, however, resides more concretely in the One who conquers the evil One. We focus on the One who is led into temptation but demonstrates faithfulness and strength that no evil can overtake. Jesus refuses to yield to the proposed momentary delights put before him. He rejects what would prevent him from praise of the one true God, the same

God who bids us welcome all life long, the One whom we approach, year after year, with a renewed spirit during Lent. He urges us onward, as if to beckon us forth with the words, "Come home, my children, come home!"

- *What was your week like last week? How might you pause this week to praise the one true God?*
- *Ah, the tempter looms. Lent has barely begun, and already you may feel confused or tempted by "that favorite foible." How might your worship with others keep you focused along your journey? Can your parish be a source of support for you these next few weeks? How?*

Renewing Your Life of Faith

The support of the church extends to all who seek faith and life. Indeed, the first Sunday of Lent offers an opportunity for remembering and for celebrating prayerfully people's movement toward God in their lives.

There is talk today of affirming faith, of ongoing conversion, of gathering with others from the diocese with the bishop in prayer. What celebration is this? It has to do with, among others, two realities: election and conversion. The latter you probably expect to hear about in Lent. But election?

The "elect" are those moving forward to baptism, confirmation and eucharist at Easter. During the celebration of election and ongoing conversion, a variety of people comes together: for example, those preparing for immersion in the Easter sacraments; many already baptized desiring to become Catholic; and many parishioners, like you, who support in prayer and action others' formation in faith.

You may ask, "I'm already baptized. Why must I concern myself with this?"

Our prayer is a prayer of the whole church for the benefit of the entire church. Sound confusing? We are a church that gathers *together*, proclaims the word *together*, worships *together* and serves *together*. God saves a people with the gracious gift of his Son to and for all humanity.

Renew your faith today by imagining yourself on a threshold, on any bridge linking life's past to present, or present to future.

Imagine yourself knowing Christ and his teaching; experiencing conversion to the gospel; forming a life of faith with an understanding of what it is to belong to the church; and desiring to be immersed in the waters of new birth, sealed with the gift of the Holy Spirit and welcomed to share at the table of the Lord. This is part of what the elect (elected by God, accepted by the church) are experiencing as they anticipate the events of Easter. However, it is a certainty that they cannot move ahead alone, nor be left alone after Easter. What god would give us birth and abandon us? Surely not the God of Abraham and Sarah, Isaac and Rebecca, Zechariah and Elizabeth.

Your spiritual preparation during Lent is not just a time, then, to renew yourself, but to do so by assisting others who are approaching *your* community as part of the bridge to this new life in Christ. The God who calls, seeks you—*your* faith, *your* warmth, *your* presence—to be Christ to these persons entrusted to the care of the already baptized. These new companions in faith cross over into the time of spiritual reflection and prayer of the church community confident that you and others are there for them—in a word, as their bridge to baptism.

As Lent begins and as the season continues, explore your ongoing sense of conversion—of a change, however small, in the way you seek and witness to the divine in your life—and know through your self-examination the saving power of God in all you do.

Use the following questions to aid your reflection.

- *What weaknesses in your life must you work on now? What needs healing in your life?*
- *What is it about your spirituality, your inner strength, your life that needs to be strengthened further? How might you pursue your parish's support of you as you offer your support to others?*

Accepting the Challenge

Breath of life, gracious gift. You are near the end of this reflection on the first Sunday of Lent. Reflect on this chapter during your spiritual journey of the next seven days. Look forward to next week, but not without focusing now on the gracious gift that is yours in Christ Jesus, the Lord.

The breath of life is a breath that sustains your living in discipleship with other believers. It is a breath that enables you to accept the gift of new life won for us all by Jesus and to move beyond limitations and fears to new vistas of faith and hope. It is a breath that itself is a gift; indeed, the Holy Spirit is the great gift promised by Jesus to his disciples. The gracious gift of God to us is a gift *of life for life*—a timeless life of union with Father, Son and Holy Spirit.

As you gather for eucharist each week, or perhaps more often during this season, explore your relationship with Jesus. Make his call to discipleship your own as you demonstrate in word and action your acceptance of God's gracious gift. Synchronize your breathing, praying with every breath, even unconsciously, the reality of Jesus as Lord and Giver of life.

Observe with keen attentiveness the gift that other people's lives are to you as they offer by *their* lively faith rich ways of living the virtues of faith, hope and charity day by day. Pray daily in praise of the Creator God, our loving Father who gives us his Son and breath of new life in the Holy Spirit.

During this Lent, pause to explore the idea that you are not really dried off from the baptismal waters of new birth, but only now perhaps are emerging from the waters of faith. Be confident that others are present to hold you up and to keep you close to that beating heart called the parish.

Prayer for the Week

Praised be the Father,
    Creator of all.
Praised be the Son,
    who offers himself for all humanity.
Praised be the Holy Spirit,
    breathing now in me
    as surely as my heart serves as constant reminder
    of God's gracious gift to me of my own life.
                        —Gerard F. Baumbach

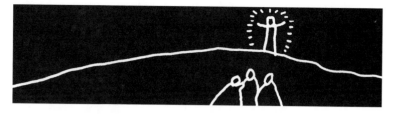

CHAPTER 2:
RADIANT BLESSING, HOLY LIFE

Second Sunday of Lent

Exploring Your Experience

Risking the unknown...a challenge to most of us, some might say. Perhaps you have faced a job transfer, a move to a healthier climate for a loved one, a move around the corner, a new farm or ranch or one of so many other possible changes. Have you ever thought of such change as something more than a risk? Would it be reasonable to hold that such a change was indeed a blessing of God? And not only a blessing, but a radiant blessing—one in and through which the majesty, wonder and mystery of God-with-us shone forth?

The work of our potter God is a divine creation, crafted out of the soil of the earth and molded by the tender hands of One far greater than the word *great* can ever capture. That "work of God" is each of us—yes, you! God masterfully creates each of us as a divine blessing, a holy work called to live the journey of this life as we glimpse with eyes of faith all that is to come.

The second Sunday of Lent encourages us to explore God's powerful call to "Blessed Abram." The constant reminder to each of us is to focus our lives on God. Oh, how easy that sounds when quickly read. If you have ever tried to focus a camera for the "perfect shot," you know how difficult it can be sometimes to bring something into focus.

As you reflect on this Lenten Sunday, renew your standing as a blessed creation of God. Identify concrete ways in which you live a holy life as a blessing of God. Does this seem impossible for you? Are you thinking, "I'm not *that* good or remarkable a person. Me, a blessed person of God? Never! I'm just not up there with the saints!" One or more of the questions that follow may assist your reflection.

- *Who is a blessing in your life? In other words, whom do you know who lives a holy life? Why would you choose this person?*
- *How might you respond to a stranger calling you, "Blessed (your name)"? What might another see in you that is a reminder to others of God's presence?*

Exploring the Scriptures

The readings for the second Sunday of Lent are:

- *Genesis 12:1–4a*
- *2 Timothy 1:8b–10*
- *Matthew 17:1–9*

How blessed are Abraham and his descendants. How blessed are we to be called to live a life that itself can be called holy. How radiant a moment to rest in the One on whom all favor finds fulfillment.

The readings for this Sunday invite reflection and action. They encourage us and challenge us to explore *who* we are, *what* we are to become, and *why* we journey in faith. With this in mind, choose one or more of the readings that follow for your reflection.

As you continue to build with your parish your Lenten-Easter bridge, remember that the Lord tells Abram, "all the communities of the earth/shall find blessing in you" (12:3). Now imagine yourself in the last twenty or thirty years of your life. You have retired from the daily grind of work, have moved perhaps to the place of your dreams and have seemingly settled into your changing, comfortable lifestyle. You may have had one or two surgical procedures along the way, suffered the loss of dear friends or even a spouse and have given your all to reconstructing a new life.

Ah, but the Lord has something new in store for you! "What?" you ask, "This cannot be, my plan is in place for my future. Please, God, let me be." God surprises you with the opportunity and adventure of a lifetime—blessing you with the chance to do divinely inspired work in a new place, and to discover all over again through your journey what faith in God is all about.

In this brief reading, the words *bless* or *blessing* appear five times. The author of Genesis captures persuasively yet gently the call of the Lord of not just Abram, but of all his descendants as well. God's call is not some bald direction—"Do this, Abram, right now...don't forget, I'm God!"—but a direction given with the promise of blessing. Not only will Abram (later Abraham) find such blessing, but the blessed presence of the Lord will be found in him by "[a]ll the communities of the earth." God blesses, as God loves, unconditionally.

This call is repeated today in your parish, your diocese, the universal church, and in your family life as well. God does not leave us alone; his love for us is too great to even fathom such a possibility.

- *How can you be a blessing this week to another person? What circumstance might present itself for you to demonstrate Christian discipleship this way?*
- *When do you need to let go? When do you know something is the right thing to do, but you cannot shake your reluctance to find blessing in the unknown?*

2 Timothy 1:8b–10

What is this call to which God beckons us? Why might we sometimes feel that God is placing unjust demands on us?

The second letter of Paul to Timothy offers rich yet sobering reflection on such questions as these. We are reminded that God calls us "to a holy life," a life that can be for us sign and enactment of the gift to us of Christ Jesus the Lord. We do not "earn" this distinction, nor do we assume that it is well deserved because of our seemingly good nature. Rather, the gift of God's life to us in Jesus, the Savior, is a freely given gift that penetrates our very being, enlivening our soul with the resolve to live a life of holiness.

"A life of holiness? I don't have time for such nonworldly matters. That's the business of priests, sisters, brothers, deacons, bishops, the pope and—well, you know—those lay people who work for the church." Is this an attitude or observation that you are familiar with? Have you heard it in your parish?

The reality is that each of us *is* called to live a life of holiness. To assert otherwise would be to limit the gospel only to those whom we assume are specially graced by God.

One key to unraveling the mystery of holiness might well be in the first sentence of this reading: "Bear your share of hardship for the gospel...." In bearing hardships, one demonstrates what holiness is about at its core. One can discover the meaning of blessing in hardship, confident that God accompanies the sufferer in and through the just and gentle hands of the local church community. The reading, after all, reminds Timothy to bear his *share* of the hardship he must face.

The radiance of the blessing of God, everpresent in hard

times and good times, glimmers anew with each passing day. Indeed, all day long God asserts his divine presence to us. The hardship that so often accompanies believers' faithful living in discipleship to Jesus Christ is not to be borne alone, but together with the support of parish and friends. We live for Christ, suffer with Christ and proclaim the mystery of Christ alive in our hearts.

- *Who might need your support in bearing hardship as she or he lives the blessing of God? Whom might you seek out to support you?*
- *How is your parish a "blessing of God"? What or who assists your parish to bear the burdens of being a light to the surrounding community at this point in time?*

Matthew 17:1–9

God gifts us with the perfect blessing and model of holiness in his Son, the Lord Jesus Christ. Jesus is blessing for all time, in all time, beyond all time, in the fullness of time. He is holiness present and fulfilled. He is the beloved Son on whom God's favor rests.

The gospel message for today is one of transfiguration. Radiant and holy blessing, Jesus is transfigured before the disciples Peter, James and John. The voice from the cloud proclaims the favor of the Lord on the beloved Son. No wonder Peter asserts how good it is for them to be with Jesus! Wouldn't you?

Jesus is the blessing of God in the flesh. He does not represent God, nor does he only say things that appear to be "God-like"; rather, he is the very presence of God among us. He is truly Emmanuel, God with us. How wonderful that Moses and

Elijah are identified in the passage; Jesus does not come ignoring all that has gone before, but makes all things new in himself.

Jesus invites Peter, James, John—yes, and us—to witness what holiness and blessing are to be. He offers himself in this graced moment; later, in his journey with the cross, he will offer himself again in another graced moment. And all the while, he assures his disciples that they need not be afraid.

- *The voice from the clouds in this passage says, "[L]isten to him." How might you be more attentive to the call of Jesus in your life?*
- *When do you actively listen to people who are today's prophets? How do you free your mind of distractions? How attentive are you to our bishops as our teachers?*

Renewing Your Life of Faith

Have you ever felt that you had secured your place in the kingdom of God and that nothing could ever challenge your resolve to be a faithful disciple? But then something happens, perhaps unexplained, and you struggle to maintain the intensity of your commitment.

Lent-Easter time is an especially powerful time of challenge and resolve. During this time, we begin with a renewed spirit, radiantly blessed by Christ, our model of holiness. The ashes that symbolize the beginning of these ninety days remind us of past beginnings, present need and future glory.

Our journey in and toward holiness necessitates developing a penitential spirit. What does this mean? If we look to the liturgy of the church, we find some helpful insight. People baptized in other churches seeking to become Catholic or Catholic people seeking confirmation and eucharist are offered this particular day during the Lenten season to focus even more clearly on their need for Christ in their lives. Part of this time of the church's prayer is for ongoing discernment of the presence of Christ and the need to avoid whatever would separate us from the love of God.

This theme is so important to the initiation of new persons into our Catholic community that it recurs, in various ways, on the next three Sundays of Lent too. But is its meaning intended to be limited only to those preparing to share for the first time in the Easter sacraments?

The prayer of the church is prayed not only in your parish or diocese, but throughout the world, a world in need of healing and hope. It is a prayer of a common faith rendered powerfully alive by the witness of all the people of God. In the prayer of the church, you see the welcoming embrace of a community of faith that cherishes *all* its members while depending on the prayer, example and participation of people like yourself. Pause here to explore the following.

- *What did you struggle with last week? What might you do this week should this situation happen again? When might you pray?*
- *How can you affirm a family member or other person as a blessing of God during this week? What simple situation might present itself for you to do this?*

Accepting the Challenge

How wonderful it is to be called to a blessed life! We are linked to Abraham and his descendants, gifted by God with being signs of his blessing to others.

Remember that an underlying attitude of rejoicing can

shape one's whole life, despite the trials and pitfalls one may encounter. You may be challenged by a sudden family illness, loss of a job, lack of purpose in life, lack of communication between yourself and a parent or yourself and a child.

Whatever your challenge, rest peacefully and confidently in the blessing God offers you. The point is not to accept blindly whatever challenges you, but to know at the core of what you are becoming the abiding presence of the God who comes...of the God who penetrates our humanity with the blessed and radiant One. Such an awareness enables you to grow in holiness and wholeness as your entire being, body and soul, rests in the presence of God—not only during Lent, but all year long.

With Christ at the center of your life, for now and forever, you meet challenges that come your way confident that you are not alone. Christ, the Beloved Son, comes to you in all the ways you may have become accustomed to, and in ways not yet imagined. He surprises you, perhaps, through the hands and voices of the most unlikely of people who cross your path each day. He sustains you in work, cradles you in crises, nourishes you in eucharist.

The God who comes in the fullness of time and calls us to such a rich life offers us his own Son in birth, death and resurrection. Surely, it is good for us to be living in this time of new life! How wise, then, it is for us to do as the voice from the cloud proclaims, "Listen to him." In the listening and the living, we glimpse and become a holy people, radiantly blessed for all eternity.

- *During the coming week, explore who it is who reminds you of the radiant blessing of God in your life. Who is such a sign to you?*

Prayer for the Week

Loving Lord, thank you
    for the gift of your blessing in my life,
    for the radiance that surrounds me each day,
    for the brilliance of all that you give me through the
        hearts
        hands
        voices and
        eyes
        of your people.
Lord, I seek holiness of life,
    so that I may offer my life as gift to you.
Help me, Lord, that I may hear your call
    and always listen to you,
    the eternal Blessed One, now and forever. Amen.
                     —*Gerard F. Baumbach*

CHAPTER 3:
THIRSTY HEARTS, WATERED SPIRITS

Third Sunday of Lent

Exploring Your Experience

What power is this, that we are so much in awe of its strength? What images surface as we consider the power and wonder of water, that rich symbol of our entrance into the new life of Christ? To help you explore the power of water, read the following story.

The Valley

The fresh mountain air was moist from several rainfalls that had drenched the picturesque Pennsylvania valley. It had been sunny and warm earlier in the month, but now dark and ominous skies threatened to saturate the valley once again.

Who would have expected the river that snaked its way through the valley to swell to such proportions that not even the enormous dikes could contain the raging waters? Sirens signaled a call to evacuate, to move to higher ground. The valley would become a swampland unless the river could be contained.

Many volunteers loaded sandbags to shore up the dikes. Hour after hour bags were filled and piled high. Workers formed teams, taking breaks more frequently as exhaustion set in. The river, however, would not be denied, and the barrier eventually surrendered to the powerful onslaught.

For three days the water rose. Slowly, deliberately, it engulfed the valley. River towns became underwater villages. Some parts of the valley were cut off from neighboring communities, inundated by overflowing creeks. Later, people watched and waited as the river slowly receded from the valley's homes. It had demonstrated its awesome power—blanketing the area under twenty feet of water. All that was left was a valley-wide path of mud and debris, with homes shaken from their foundations.

During this rampaging storm, the spirit of the people of this hidden valley held up. They worked together to survive and seemingly to say, "Water, we shall absorb your power, tire from your might, but sustain ourselves and go on living with one another's strength."

The people of this community rallied around a common purpose, and demonstrated in working together a spirit capable of overcoming even the worst adversity. As one editorial from the *Wilkes-Barre Times Leader* put it: "We will rebuild to a better future, supported by our friends here and outside the area, and with faith in our own spirit and with faith in God."

• *Take a walk during the next few days. Quietly observe several ways in which water is used. When you return home, identify some ways you depend on water in your home. As you walk and after you return home, think about ways in which you may take this life-sustaining and life-destroying liquid for granted. In what ways do you not?*

Exploring the Scriptures

The third Sunday of Lent begins a group of three great Lenten Sundays. On these Sundays the church treats several themes that offer us a sharpened glimpse of the meaning of the paschal mystery—the mystery of Christ's passion, death, resurrection and finally his ascension. For it is now that we explore themes of living water, light and life. Not surprisingly, as we explore the intersection of such common human elements with the life of grace, we begin to discover more about who we are and what we are becoming as disciples of the risen Christ.

The readings for the third Sunday of Lent are:

- *Exodus 17:3-7*
- *Romans 5:1-2, 5-8*
- *John 4:5-42*

Exodus 17:3-7

Have you ever left a place in haste, frightened and puzzled, only to yearn for what you left after you had gained your freedom? This is the situation facing Moses in this passage from Exodus. Moses puts his life on the line and leads his people in their desert journey, only to hear their grumbling about having been "made" to leave Egypt; they yearn for the way things used to be. They think it was better. They thirst. Hardened hearts surely thirst, don't they? But for what do the Israelites really thirst?

Moses challenges the Lord. He is frustrated and fearful—he may even be stoned by the ones saved by the power of God. He does what the Lord commands, and this is the thanks he gets? One might imagine Moses doing more than challenging God!

Moses, the leader who had overcome the power of water, now finds in this same power a way to satisfy the thirst of his people. He does what God commands, and water bursts forth from the rock. God saves a people...over and over and over—even and always in the midst of their quarrelsome ways. Yes, even when hearts are hardened.

Do we sometimes "test" God? Do we become edgy with some event or plan, unwilling to seek and see the wisdom of God in what is before us? Now explore the following.

- *How might you listen for the voice of God in your midst? What might help you to develop a listening heart, one that thirsts always for the living God?*
- *Who in your parish seems to be able to move above quarrelsome ways, get to the heart of an important matter and bring about understanding? Why is that?*

Romans 5:1–2, 5–8

Although we may sometimes be encouraged to pray "in the quiet of our hearts," the speaker probably does not intend to imply that our hearts are to be silent. With "the love of God...poured out into our hearts/through the Holy Spirit...," how could our hearts ever be silent? Rather, they are rich in the wisdom of God, ripening our faith so that, like an impatient child, we cannot wait to share the message of Christ with others.

There is just so much at stake here. The love of Christ pours forth into our hearts; the Holy Spirit pierces our humanity with the fire of new hope, calling us to be disciples of Jesus Christ, and challenging us to remain strong in steadfast love when we are weakened. We are confident in our hope in the One who died for us, the risen One.

Water and heart—two essential aspects of our identity as Christian people. These clearly human aspects of what makes us living beings become for us symbolic of the movement of God—Father, Son and Holy Spirit—in our everyday lives. God comes to us in many ways, including the natural flow and rhythm of events in our lives. Perhaps we need to reflect on how we continue to respond to God's compelling call.

- *Think of your heart, its chambers, its activity as that conduit of energy throughout your body. What might result if your heart becomes hardened? How might you prevent this from happening? On whom do you rely to support you?*

John 4:5–42

For some of us, this gospel is known as the first of the "long Lenten gospels." One can almost see the passion account of Palm Sunday around the corner. With added length to these passages, some surmise that something even more important is happening as we wander—but not aimlessly—through the word of God.

This classic gospel account from John beckons us to the water theme again, this time at a well. The passage is particularly meaningful for those preparing for baptism. At the well, Jesus begins a conversation with a Samaritan woman who has come to draw water. For Jesus to speak with a Samaritan, and a woman, is no small matter. The Jews and Samaritans of Jesus' day were not on speaking terms. Jesus does something that simply is not to be done. But he has strong reason for what he does. He came for *all* people.

Jesus thirsts, he tells the woman. She is puzzled that Jesus, a Jew, would even approach her for a drink. But Jesus speaks of living water, the gift of God to the woman at the well and to all who thirst. He speaks of never being thirsty again: "[T]he water I shall give will become in him/a spring of water welling up to eternal life." Ordinary water satisfies for a moment; living water satisfies for eternity.

Jesus then queries her lifestyle, discussing the several husbands the woman has had. The woman keenly observes Jesus' interest in her spiritual welfare and speaks of the coming Messiah. The gospel does not tell us her reaction when Jesus states, "I am he, the one speaking with you." But one can imagine the fervor in her new water nourishment: she returns to her town and lets everyone know of Jesus' deep insight into her life and his compassion for her situation. She suggests that he may even be the Messiah.

There is so much more one could say about this passage. For our reflection here, it is sufficient to focus on this living water—water that sustains when one sows, strengthens when another reaps and yields abundant fruit. This is the water of eternal life, intended for all. It is, indeed, the living water of life in the One who will say shortly before his death, "I thirst." The woman at the well becomes a well-woman, saved and renewed by the Jewish teacher who asks for no more than a drink, but in dialogue demonstrates himself as the living and eternal source of wellness. Jesus is our living water.

Through Jesus' word to others, people come to believe in him. How do we not only come to faith but grow in faith? What "well" do we use to stop and talk to Jesus? To dig beneath the surface of our being and risk exposure of our innermost secrets?

Jesus urges us to rest in this living water, live in it, nurture our children in it, care for our elderly in it. In all of this, he gives life to dry and hardened human hearts, offering us the timeless gift of eternal life. This is not some simple poetic image to make us feel good, but serious stuff for us Christians. Through this living water, we worship Father, Son and Spirit. The living Lord moves us through space and time, God-with-us in a momentary glimpse of all that is to come.

- *Imagine yourself in the vicinity of the well. You see Jesus and the Samaritan woman. Are you horrified? Are you a Samaritan yourself? A woman? A man? Are you thirsty? Do you try to overhear their conversation and as you listen wonder if Jesus' probing interest might shift to you? What might you do?*

Renewing Your Life of Faith

During this third week of Lent, the church again reminds us of our journey with the entire people of God. We pray especially for those journeying toward the Easter sacraments and link our fasting and almsgiving to theirs in this time of personal and parish renewal.

The word that envelops us during this time is a word of healing and forgiveness, selflessness and sanctity. It is the word of God, unable to be constrained or held back by all who are able to hear. For us as people of faith, this word captures our whole being, heart and soul. It is truly the word for the thirsty.

We see these themes come together during special times of prayer celebrated with those seeking baptism, now called the elect. The elect are people in their final weeks of spiritual preparation before baptism. Lent is a retreat time for them as well as the entire parish.

The church will celebrate three special prayer times with the elect, on the third, fourth and fifth Sundays of Lent. The word used to describe each of these special times of prayer is "scrutiny." The scrutinies are opportunities to contemplate where their hearts are struggling, as well as to search out what might be strengthened along the path to Easter.

During mass on this Sunday, and after several prayers of intercession on behalf of all the elect, the celebrant prays that their hearts be receptive to the Lord Jesus. They must be assured that, even as they are dismissed to explore the word with catechumenate team members, their sisters and brothers in faith continue to pray for them during the liturgy of the eucharist.

The elect need the witness and prayer of the gathered community. We need to be people who witness both by our common prayer and individual behavior. Each of us can help to bring them to the saving well of baptism, encouraging them all along the way with an attitude that proclaims in word and action, "Yes, your thirst will be satisfied." We can water them, and all those preparing for reception into the church, with the spirit of our love, friendship and good will. At Easter, they will thirst no more.

- *How is your parish a sign of support to others? Is it in need of healing and forgiveness?*
- *What might you do this week as a sign of your care for those preparing for baptism or entrance into the Catholic Church? How might you "water their spirits" and keep watch, lest they be overcome by the evil One?*

Accepting the Challenge

In the early centuries of the church, those coming to faith were urged to commit to memory the truths of faith, known to us today as the profession of faith, or creed. This was living truth, and the concern was not for writing it down, but "engraving it by memory on the heart" (Cyril of Jerusalem). The truth of faith was to be kept as an essential dimension of what one would need to live as a Christian all life long.

Today we need these truths of faith no less than they were needed centuries ago. The profession of faith summarizes the truths of God's revelation to us. These truths help satisfy the thirst of our minds and hearts for knowing and living by the sacred mysteries professed by the church.

Often during this third week of Lent, the creed is presented to those seeking baptism. In just a few weeks, on Holy Saturday, they will recite the creed; at the Easter vigil, they will profess their firmly rooted faith.

Our spiritual quest is enlivened by sharing in common with our sisters and brothers these core beliefs of the Christian community. This profession of the mysteries of our faith is another great sign of all that God offers us, the already baptized and those preparing for baptism. The truths professed challenge *all* to be faithful to the ongoing call of discipleship.

We are immersed in the love of God and watered by the Holy Spirit, the One who saturates our spirits with the blessedness of gentle and healing hearts, not fractured or hardened ones. Our hearts thirst for the living God, our spirits yearn for the water that yields new life in Christ.

Will you pursue the spiritual journey, perhaps without knowing the risks involved? Or might you seek shelter in spiritual routine, avoiding the risks at hand, perhaps keeping yourself safe but not necessarily secure? May the gift of faith, the gift to a thirsty heart, provide your response. And may the Holy Spirit water your own spirit with the power and wonder of the sacred mysteries of faith in Jesus Christ.

Prayer for the Week

Loving God,
    you give us the gift of your Son
    as living water.
Move our hearts to respond to the promptings
    of the Holy Spirit
    so that we may risk and not run
    pray without ceasing
    love without fear
    journey with confidence
    and testify to your eternal word.
Dear Lord, you satisfy every hunger, every thirst.
    Be with us as we urge others to taste these
        sacred waters
    and know forever
        the wonders of your love. Amen.
                        —*Gerard F. Baumbach*

CHAPTER 4:
PROBING LORD, ABIDING LIGHT

Fourth Sunday of Lent

Exploring Your Experience

Shallow. Empty. Hollow.

Do you ever hear words such as these used to describe—without compliment, of course—other people? Oh, you may not hear them spoken of people *you* know well, but you may hear them from the lips of people in the media, newscasters, on television shows or in conversations at work. Perhaps not intended to defame another person, such terms often represent a rush to judgment (more likely, a rash judgment) about an innocent third party.

What makes people assume such characteristics of others? Why do we sometimes hear about, or fall into ourselves, the practice of seemingly dismissing others?

Perhaps we fail to probe, to go beneath the surface of what others bring to us. We may miss the obvious, assuming that what is before us is as unclear as a bog on a humid summer night. One would be a bit fearful of entering such uncharted foggy territory! However, sometimes we pass through the moving mist with surprising ease and wonder why so much energy was spent on what had appeared to be an enormous challenge only moments before.

Through the mist we begin to see clearly the person

labeled...*shallow...empty...hollow*. Oh, how we wish we could avoid such judgment and welcome always the Lord's direction captured by the Psalmist: "[B]eside restful waters he leads me;.../He guides me in right paths..." (Psalm 23:1–3).

As the Lord probes beneath the very recesses of our lives, he approaches as abiding light. He is not some supernatural doctor, probing with an instrument, searching for what is unknown. No, Christ comes to us as shepherd, calmly calling us to himself, lighting the way as we journey through "right paths." Take a few moments now for reflection.

- *When are you most apt to surrender to our probing Lord? When might you choose to overcome influences that urge you to "do it all on my own"?*
- *What path are you traveling now? Do you see this path as the way of the Lord in your life? Might you need to probe deeper and seek a new direction?*

Exploring the Scriptures

The Light of the world brightens our journey through Lent and all year long. He sees what is within and beckons us to demonstrate the fruits of discipleship, living in the light of faith. We do not wander aimlessly in the light, but with others by our side in mutual support, love and hope.

The readings for the fourth Sunday of Lent are:

- *1 Samuel 16:1b, 6–7, 10–13a*
- *Ephesians 5:8–14*
- *John 9:1–41*

1 Samuel 16:1b, 6–7, 10–13a

The reading opens with the words, "The LORD said to Samuel:..." Samuel, judge of Israel, is chosen by God to approach the shepherd Jesse of Bethlehem to seek out and anoint with oil the one who would serve someday as king of God's chosen ones.

These were changing times for the people of Israel, a time of movement from rule by tribal judges (of whom Samuel is the last) to a time of monarchy (with Saul, anointed by Samuel, as the first king). Despite Samuel's concerns about making the journey to Bethlehem, the Lord assures him that the one to be anointed will be found there.

Jesse offers seven sons, but Samuel, seeking to do the will of God, probes a bit more. He seeks not the seven presented, but the youngest of all, David, destined to become king of all Israel. The Lord does not make the first or most obvious choice, but has Samuel pursue the one he seeks, for "the LORD looks into the heart" (16:7). He seeks David, the least obvious and most surprising choice—after all, he was out tending sheep when God chose him! Perhaps Samuel could have gone for the best dressed, most polite, most politic, most vivacious personality. But no, God has other plans.

What might we gain from this passage for our lives today? The Lord probes our hearts, seeking to uncover what may be hidden even to ourselves—and certainly to others. The Lord surprises us with choices that may appear to be the opposite of what we might prefer. What we see before us might challenge even our faith as we seek to do the Lord's will in our lives.

The passage concludes with "the spirit of the LORD rushed upon David" (16:13). Are we ready for the "rush of the Spirit" during this Lenten time? Or are we "control freaks," willing to say yes to God, but only when *we* are ready? After all, what if the rush of the Spirit should happen when we are busy with shopping, recreational activities or working? Can we afford to risk the inconvenience?

Can we afford not to? What does the Lord see as he looks into our hearts? Are we receptive? Welcoming? Fearful? Anxious?

Guilt-ridden? The God of Samuel and David pierces our hearts with love, an eternal and abiding tenderness that swells beyond anything we could ever imagine.

- *This week, ponder the movement of God in your heart. Know his gentle and probing presence, calling you to listen, to act, to live as his own child. Know the abiding presence of our saving God in the rush of the Spirit all week long.*

Ephesians 5:8–14

Images of probing may lead to images of darkness; for example, how might you find your way when in total darkness? Yes, you explore gingerly, you move slowly as you probe the unknown surroundings.

Paul moves beyond being "in darkness" in this reading. He likens the Ephesians to darkness itself, reminding them that once they *were* darkness. Now they are "light in the Lord" (5:8). Those asleep in faith must rise with the risen One, and be people who not only light the way but become that abiding light of Christ for all to see.

The light that is ours not only brightens our day but exposes what is evil in our time. There is no hiding from this eternal light. There is no mountain so large that it can cast a shadow over evil to which people may yield, or even to which they may succumb. This can be a hard message for some people, whose slumber in faith may need to be jolted back to that reality which is Christ, the eternal Word.

- *How might your parish demonstrate to those preparing for the Easter sacraments that we live in the light of Christ? That the light of Christ that will engulf our church during the vigil of Easter can never be extinguished?*

John 9:1–41

One of the great gospels of the Lenten season is today's, for it is here that we explore further the notions of light, of blindness, of openness to the Savior of the world. The account of the man born blind is the way this passage is usually identified.

Notice that Jesus uses an earthy act—that of mixing his saliva with dirt—to make the muddy substance to cover the man's eyes. Listening to Jesus, the man goes and washes. His blindness is gone. But is our only interest here physical blindness? Or is there a greater blindness?

The one who now can see interacts with neighbors, with those who were used to observing his begging ways and with Pharisees. He is met with varying degrees of acceptance of Jesus' healing act. Jesus boldly ministers to this person on the sabbath, prompting the Pharisees to object to what he does. As we see in the passage, his parents are called upon to testify that he has been blind from birth. Again, emphasis on the "clear facts of the case."

But why such stress on blindness here? The Light of the world knows no limits, and Jesus is such light to the man blind from birth. The man listens to his healer, his source of light.

When questioned, the enlightened and straightforward man identifies Jesus as a prophet. The one healed affirms what has been done to and for him, and even asks his questioners if they also wish to become Jesus' disciples. One can imagine the displeasure with which this suggestion was met! They do not really hear all about which he testifies. Perhaps he is really inviting them to be healed of their own blindness.

What follows is another powerful encounter with Jesus. The

newly enlightened man responds with words we use even today ("I do believe, Lord") in affirming his belief in the One who both *is* light and *brings* light.

Sadly, some who "see" today on the outside (that is, with their eyes) are blinded to this light. They see only on the surface, whisking by life's divine agenda, not probing beneath what shields them from the Son of God. From the earth, the soil of God's creation, Jesus heals, enlightens and opens us to his abiding presence among us. Oh, great and abiding Light of Christ, Light of the world, give us your Spirit to guide our way!

- *Can you be light to another person this week? A family member, friend or colleague at work? What should you do?*

Renewing Your Life of Faith

The phrase "probing Lord, abiding light" helps us to focus on what we are about during these middle days of Lent. We are well into the Lord's movement in our hearts; with the cycle of each day, from sunrise to sunset and to sunrise again, we live in the abiding presence of the Lord. During Lent especially, we probe and listen to God's word with those preparing for the Easter sacraments.

During the fourth Lenten Sunday, we celebrate the second scrutiny with the elect. Imagine for a moment their growing anticipation, and even anxiety, over what they are about to do. In just three weeks they will be immersed in the waters of new birth, be confirmed in the Holy Spirit and come to the table of the eucharist for the first time. How wonderful it is that the entire church joins them as they walk these last days of reflection and contemplation before the celebration of their new birth—in the presence of you, their sister or brother in faith.

The second scrutiny is another prayer of the church, the people of God. Our elect do not stand alone, but probe the depths of their hearts with the support of people like you, bearers of the light of Christ, the already baptized. The gospel for this Sunday provides the scriptural focus for the second scrutiny. Our common prayer is one of continued strength for the elect. We pray that they will see with eyes of faith, in the mystery in which they are being immersed, the light to live their lives as witnesses to the Lord Jesus Christ.

Your continued support of those preparing for Easter sacraments can be a sign to them of God's abiding presence lived out in your parish community. The parish is your home and theirs, and is a vital dimension to growth in faith for all God's people.

If you are fortunate enough to participate in the celebration of a scrutiny, the experience can be a crisp reminder of what it is you value and hold dear as a Catholic. The prayers of the scrutiny speak of light, witness, truth, overcoming sinfulness, openness to God and much more. Moment after moment, word after word, ritual action after ritual action, we pray in the abiding presence of the risen One. The Holy Spirit, alive in your heart, burns also in the elect, moving all this Lent to embrace the cross of the One who lights our way, the Light of the world.

- *When you hear the homilist speak of faithfulness to the gospel of Christ, imagine how seriously this message is received by those seeking baptism. What example do they give for those of us who are already baptized?*
- *How might the Light of Christ light your way this week? Will you call on the Lord? Will you seek out this light, even when things are going well?*
- *Who is the light of Christ to you today? Does your choice surprise you? What did you expect?*

Accepting the Challenge

Jesus, the Light of the world, embraced the cross and set all people free. The church reminds us all Lent long of the cross of Christ, the cross that we will venerate in just a few weeks on Good Friday.

Perhaps one of the challenges we face as we grasp the cross of Christ is that of identifying the need for reconciliation in our lives. The sacrament of the same name, reconciliation, or penance, may appear to be "more popular" during Lent, as we dig deeper and assess our need to be reconciled with God and our brothers and sisters in Christ.

Are you willing to let Jesus light your way to the sacramental encounter with him in the power and beauty of God's forgiveness? Do you sense the movement of the Holy Spirit, probing your heart, moving you beyond spiritual blindness, to celebrate this sacramental mystery of the all-loving and all-merciful God?

"But wait,..." you might think, "perhaps it is too soon for me to pursue this sacrament. I have read already in this book of healing, of forgiveness, of becoming a more faithful disciple of Jesus Christ. Isn't that enough?" Some of us may even wonder why we need to bother with the sacrament of penance at all: we have good friends, radio psychologists, therapists and many other people available to us. Can't they do for us what a priest can do?

The light of Christ guides us in right paths as we approach the sacrament of reconciliation. It burns not only on the way of forgiveness but enlightens us with the recognition of the call of the Lord to be free of whatever hinders our growth in faith.

When our parish gathers for this sacrament, we have the opportunity to pray with our brothers and sisters in still another mystery of faith. We yearn to express sorrow for whatever sins we have committed and we confess them privately to the priest, "the sign and the instrument of God's merciful love for the sinner" (*Catechism*, #1465). The priest gives us a penance, a prayer or good work, for example, so that we might "make amends." It is the priest who absolves us, forgiving our sins in the name of the risen One, Jesus Christ.

After Easter, this sacrament of God's healing care will

become part of the lives of those seeking baptism, the first sacrament of forgiveness. Indeed, the elect experience the forgiveness of all sin, original and personal, in the sacrament of baptism. Following baptism, they will know, as you know now, the comforting call home of the Lord when the evil One seems, even momentarily, to cause one to drift from right paths. How much we need the abiding light of Christ!

Try to take a walk this week, just you and the Lord. Awaken early and walk (despite the weather!). Let Christ light your way with the glow of his eternal light. Invite him to pierce your heart with the power of his love. Pray for openness to the Holy Spirit as you examine your conscience, so that you may be ever faithful to the gift of baptism that is yours—a gift of new life in the mystery of the Risen Christ.

Prayer for the Week

Lord Jesus Christ,
   you light my way
   with your abiding presence.
   You probe the depths of my being and
   stay with me on right paths
   so that I remain one with you and
   all my sisters and brothers in faith.
Help us all to see whatever blinds us
   from your movement in our lives.
Help my parish to focus even more on you,
   our Savior and Lord.
Give us the grace to know the gentle rush of the
   Holy Spirit
Calling us forth to live as
   bearers of the light,
   reconcilers among all people,
   and ever faithful to the gift of our baptism. Amen.
                         —Gerard F. Baumbach

CHAPTER 5:
WEEPING LORD, SPIRIT DWELLING

Fifth Sunday of Lent

Exploring Your Experience

How do you know God is with you? Do you know God's presence in a whisper? a friend? a symphony? a spouse? a child? a family reunion? a falling tear? a parish liturgy? an illness? a rally for just wages? a homilist who touches you deeply? the rosary? a poor person? a hospital room? a wake? a wedding? a birth? a sunrise? a rainfall? evening time?

God-with-us: perhaps a phrase we all too often take for granted, for God is with us always. The Holy Spirit penetrates our being with the awesome wonder of divine life and creative presence of God in our midst.

God-with-us: yes...even when we sometimes wish—oh, perhaps with a bit of embarrassment or confusion—that God would look the other way...so we could go about our daily business and not have to rely so much on the gift of conscience, the power of the word, the call to justice, the wisdom of the Son. After all, are there not times when "I just want to do what I want to do" and not worry about "eternal consequences"?

But it doesn't work that way for the Christian, does it? The loving God of all creation yearns for our return, beckons us to faithfulness, in fact dwells in us and brings us to life. The Holy

Spirit is with those who otherwise would be dead, now come to life in the death and resurrection of Jesus Christ.

What keeps you alert to the Holy Spirit? Is it just coincidence when you sense that something appears to you to be the work of God in your life?

The Lord of all creates, pursues, dwells within, sustains and lifts us up. Words fail to capture God's presence in our life...how can we describe such burning and eternal love? How can we even imagine such deep immersion in the life of God-with-us?

- *What memory do you have of an especially meaningful religious experience? Close your eyes, breathe softly and be aware of the presence of God deep within your soul. Recall the experience...the people...the surroundings...the smells... the sights...the holy.... How was this experience a blessing for you or for others?*

Exploring the Scriptures

The readings for the fifth Sunday of Lent are:

- *Ezekiel 37:12–14*
- *Romans 8:8–11*
- *John 11:1–45*

As you discover some new insight or renew that which you already know during your reflection, consider God's nearness to you in every aspect of your being. Know again God's attentiveness to you, his kindness, forgiveness and his dwelling within you and the entire community of the church. Be full of life as you uncover now that radiant gift of our all-good God. Trust in the God who sustains you in baptism, nourishes you in eucharist and directs your living justly in all the moments of your life.

Ezekiel 37:12–14

"O my people!"

The prophet Ezekiel sounds forth the word of the Lord with these simple words, probably vigorously delivered. They are words that embrace the listener, words that pierce the hearts of God's own people. They are a call to hope, to hold fast together and know that the chains that bind will be loosed.

The God of rebirth is near.

In this passage, Ezekiel's words are directed to a people in exile. They had been sent into exile from the southern kingdom of Judah, which had been overtaken by the Babylonians. The period of this exile from their homeland is dated from 587 to 538 before Christ. (The northern kingdom, Israel, had already fallen to the Assyrians more than a century before.) Living in a foreign land, they yearned for the land of their temple, for that holy ground of God's watchful presence.

Yet, did not Ezekiel prophesy about the sinfulness of his people *before* the exile? "The people of the land practice extortion and commit robbery; they afflict the poor and the needy, and oppress the resident alien without justice" (22:29).

How forgiving the Lord God is! The Lord God promises to "put my spirit in you that you may live...." As God resides in his people, so will they reside in the land to which they seek to return. There is no room for sinfulness here.

For now, however, these people are foreigners; in fact, for children born of the exile there are only the memories of parents and their Jewish community on which to depend. Their beginning experience as God's chosen ones occurs on foreign soil.

How are they to live? What is expected of these people in bondage? Perhaps we could ask ourselves similar questions. How might each of us, and with one another in our parish community, live for God? How do we, individually and as a community, affirm the dignity of every living person? of people who are especially vulnerable (including, perhaps, ourselves)?

As God's presence settles upon the land of his people, so may it settle in us. The promise of the Lord is an irrevocable commitment, a covenant love that cannot be contained.

- *Who are the poor in your life? the vulnerable? the resident alien?*
- *What might you do to show solidarity with them this Lent?*

Romans 8:8–11

Our attention in this reading is directed to the Holy Spirit. Paul tells the Romans that the Holy Spirit dwells within them; one so filled belongs to Christ. It is the Holy Spirit who gives life and enables just living.

The passage is one of the classic scriptural passages about the Holy Spirit. Because Paul made the distinction between flesh and spirit, we can learn an important lesson from his insight. In everything one does, the believer transformed by the Holy Spirit lives for the greater glory of God. One's physical life—with its limitations, with its fall to sin—is seen in relation to life in the spirit. This spirit-life is an experience of God within, of the Holy Spirit prompting the whole person to a belonging that can only be satisfied in Christ.

"[T]he Spirit of the one who raised Jesus from the dead" is one with us. There is no room for sinfulness here. The Holy Spirit rests within you, raising you to walk in the newness of life. God gives strength to the weary, hope to the vanquished, love to those called to proclaim the presence of the Holy Spirit that imbues the community of faith with the gift of life, the gift of grace.

The Holy Spirit dwells within the church and each of us. Our belonging to Christ happens in communion with our sisters and brothers in faith, and beckons us forth to invite others to belong with us.

How do we craft this invitation to others? What evidence of our lives enables people to see Christ? To sense that he is present in this life, this parish, this community?

You might ask yourself during your Lenten reflection this week how you welcome newcomers into your parish. Remember, you are so close to Holy Week now. Imagine the feelings of one of the elect or one who is about to be received into the church. What part do you have to play in helping these people stay the course and become, through hands tightly joined, part of your parish's ongoing witness to the indwelling Holy Spirit?

- *Are you seeking a new direction, a new way of discovering the Holy Spirit who dwells within you? If so, what might this direction be?*

John 11:1–45

Do you recall last Sunday's gospel? We saw there the story of the man born blind, and the disciples' quizzical question of Jesus, inquiring whether the man's sin or that of his parents was the cause of his blindness. Jesus links the disciples' question to making manifest "the works of God" (John 9:3).

In the gospel passage for today, we read about the works of God truly made manifest once more. Through sickness, God's glory is revealed. Death is no end; resurrection is its nemesis and conqueror. In Jesus we know resurrection and life. In him is the promise of the Father, now fully revealed.

The gospel passage tells us that Lazarus, friend of Jesus and brother to Martha and Mary, women whom Jesus also loved, has died as a result of illness. The body of Lazarus is now in its fourth day of rest in the burial cave. Our weeping Lord approaches the cave of Lazarus in Bethany. Remember that, upon hearing of Lazarus's illness, Jesus waits to travel; in fact, his disciples urge him not to go, for fear of persecution by his enemies.

Fear, sickness and death do not overcome Jesus at this point. Rather, love does. Feeling the pain of the bereaved Martha and Mary, and his own as well, Jesus approaches the tomb. He calls Lazarus forth and charges the kind people who had offered Martha consolation to free him from the wrappings that envelop his body. Lazarus is free of the ties that bind.

There is much to ponder in this scriptural account, surely more than can be offered here. Jesus declares to Martha that he is both "the resurrection and the life" and offers himself to all as the way to life, despite natural death. The key is believing in Jesus Christ.

The account also poignantly and gently reveals to us our troubled, weeping Lord. Fully divine as well as fully human, Jesus experiences human love. He thanks the Father of all for hearing him; Jesus is clearly focused on bringing to the forefront God's glory. His call to Lazarus to come forward from the tomb is an affirmation of the glory of the eternal and living God.

All through history, God is healing and calling people to spirit-filled living. This is true of us today as well. Recall the first reading: a people in exile will know the presence of God in life-giving ways. Recall the second reading: the Spirit dwells within us.

We continue our Lenten retreat by resting in the Holy Spirit, the Spirit of life. The life we share as a community of faith is the life of Christ, the life of eternal promise. It is the life of resurrection and eternal hope. In moments of weeping, be one with our Lord Jesus Christ. Know the dwelling of God within, strengthening and empowering you to live as Christ's disciple in the practical realities you face with each new sunrise.

- *How might you be "Christ" to another person this week? Many of us are close to someone who suffers from serious illness. How might you be a source of hope to this person?*

What might weeping with this person mean to him or her? to you?

Renewing Your Life of Faith

Upon hearing of Lazarus's sickness, Jesus says: "This illness is not to end in death,/but it is for the glory of God,/that the Son of God may be glorified through it." What a powerful assertion of the reality of God-with-us. We can apply this reality to our parish, also.

The church is nearing the end of Lent now. With each passing day this week, the church approaches the celebration of Passion Sunday, itself just a few days before the sacred triduum. Our parish prepares to wave the palms in praise and welcome of our king, imagining perhaps our accompanying him on his final journey—the journey to the cross.

Think for a moment of the many dimensions of your life, of such aspects as thinking, loving, reflecting, praying, doing and so on. Think of your fasting and almsgiving, your growing reliance on the Holy Spirit in your life, your welcoming the stranger with wide and just arms. (You might call this glimpse of the "whole you" your spirituality.)

Think, too, of your parish's focused and retreatlike Lenten preparation for the great Easter sacraments. And think of the healing of people's lives, wrought by the glory of God shining forth through the gift of your parish.

On this day our parish celebrates the third scrutiny with the elect. The elect are soon to join us, the "faithful," the already baptized. We pray many prayers of intercession for them and in such prayer may come to see even more clearly our own need for dwelling in God's presence ever more fervently.

Today is a day for prayer together, for shaking free from the power of death. The elect now need more than ever to drink of the strength of our witness. They need sisters and brothers to help them bridge the mysteries, to move ahead in these last days before Holy Week and the great three days of the Easter triduum.

When they look forward, they need to see you calling them to the altar of new birth.

When they look back, they need to see your witness as a firm foundation that will help to sustain them.

When they appear to be alone or troubled, puzzled or pensive, they need the gift of your presence. Remember our weeping Lord.

- *What practical gesture might you offer to do this week on behalf of one of the elect? or on behalf of a parishioner who could benefit from your listening heart?*

Gradually, perhaps, the community's seemingly repetitious focus on healing and freedom from sin becomes an ongoing opportunity for spiritual renewal for all of us. And so it is now that we renew our efforts to overcome whatever evil may prevent us from living as wise and gentle disciples of the Lord. What might we do? We can respond together to the universal call to holiness and to the new life for which death is no match.

Accepting the Challenge

Perhaps you wish you could do as the elect and those preparing for reception into the church are now doing—building a memory bank of meaningful faith experiences centered around the celebration of the Easter sacraments. After all, you may wonder, if you were baptized as an infant, what memory do you have? If confirmation and first eucharist followed years later when you were a child, how was the unity of the sacraments of initiation preserved as you grew in Catholic faith and life?

Do not dismiss quickly early childhood faith experiences. The innocence of your youthful faith was like a seedling, growing gradually over time and blossoming even now. Whatever the way you have walked on the path of new life, be aware that you are part of one communion, one body in Christ.

Your life in Christ is part of that broader life of the church. It is part of our shared history of accepting the challenge of a blossoming faith, not only years ago but also today. Discovering more along the way of new life is our daily challenge on this Lenten sunset before Easter. To do this, we pray...in word, gesture, action, quietly and together.

The prayer of the church is, of course, vital to our communion together as the body of Christ. Our worship and prayer together are like a heartbeat, keeping us alive as the people of God.

One prayer of great power, rich tradition and daily challenge is the Our Father. The Lord's Prayer is often presented to the elect during the fifth week of Lent, although it may be presented much earlier during the time of preparation, or even later, during the final prayerful preparations on Holy Saturday.

We need to remind ourselves of the journey of our elect, of their approaching immersion in the waters of new birth. Consider this verse from Paul's letter to the Romans: "For you did not receive a spirit of slavery to fall back into fear, but you received a spirit of adoption, through which we cry, *Abba,* 'Father!'" (8:15). We join our elect in offering praise to the Holy One to whom Jesus prayed as we pray the prayer Jesus gave us. *All* cry, "Abba, Father!"

We pray the Lord's Prayer with our parish in union with the whole church at every eucharistic celebration. We can pray it privately or with others wherever we are. It can be a beautiful part of our meditation as we pray the mysteries of the rosary. As you make this prayer your own, be conscious of the entire church at prayer, worldwide. Search your heart for what binds you to the community of faith in this common prayer of praise and future hope.

As you conclude this meditation, place your needs at the altar of new life. Be secure in the presence of the One who says, "I am the resurrection and the life." Seek the healing love of the Lord who wept over Lazarus and mourned with Martha and Mary. In all you do, and particularly with your parish during the three days of the triduum, rest gracefully and gratefully in the Holy Spirit.

• *The prayer suggested for the week is the Lord's Prayer. As you pray this prayer of Jesus each day this week, consider selecting a different phrase for your daily meditation. What might the Holy Spirit be leading you to uncover through these words today?*

Prayer for the Week

Our Father,
who art in heaven,
hallowed be thy name;
thy kingdom come;
thy will be done on earth
as it is in heaven.
Give us this day our daily bread;
and forgive us our trespasses
as we forgive those
who trespass against us;
and lead us not into temptation,
but deliver us from evil. Amen.

CHAPTER 6:
CHRIST JESUS, HUMBLED AND EXALTED

Passion Sunday (Palm Sunday)

Exploring Your Experience

The king is here! The Master enters the city of Jerusalem, the place that will in a few days see him struggle with a cross on the way to his death. How blessed is the prophet of God!

Somehow this may not make sense, at least not to people of today. Today's probing, ordered and objective minds may well see contradiction in Jesus of Nazareth, and especially in his final days. How can one's approaching death be called blessed?

One moment Jesus hears statements of faithfulness forever from his disciples; the next, they are asleep when he needs their presence.

One moment Jesus moves about freely among his followers; the next, he is taken into custody.

One minute crowds proclaim him prophet; the next, they shout "Let him be crucified!"

Christianity and contradiction go hand in hand. What *should* happen so often doesn't, even though we are convinced it really should. Read again the first paragraph above. The Master arrives to cries of "Hosanna" (see Mark 11:1–10 or John 12:12–16). How pleased the crowds appear to be! Yet in just a few days he will give his life, willingly, for these crowds and the crowds of time. Oh contradiction, you Christianity.

Are there contradictions in your life?

Before you judge yourself too harshly, realize that, for the Christian, contradiction is both gift and challenge. You may notice people who, in declaring their allegiance to no religious body, seem to get "all the breaks." Or a person who, in your humble opinion, is not nearly as faithful to the church as you are, is welcomed more warmly by others in your parish. Perhaps the challenge here is to refrain from passing judgment and to humbly seek the judgment of God, exposing yourself to divine wisdom, trust and love.

- *Identify some contradictions that sometimes make life difficult for you. What influences still seem to grip you tight, preventing you from letting go and trusting in the Lord?*

Exploring the Scriptures

What is your experience of sorrow? of distress? of humility? of being exalted? These are just a few of the terms used to describe Christ in today's readings. Many more could be mentioned. People have wondered for centuries, from generation to generation, about Jesus of Nazareth and his total giving of self in life and in death. Meditate on your relationship to Christ Jesus, Humble One and Exalted One as you prayerfully read today's readings.

The readings for mass on Passion Sunday are:

- *Isaiah 50:4–7*
- *Philippians 2:6–11*
- *Matthew 26:14–27:66*

Isaiah 50:4–7

Can we sing the song we find proclaimed in this reading? How are we servants of the Lord God?

We read that daily the Lord is with the suffering one, who is not abandoned by him to champions of pain and suffering. The reading enables us to make powerful linkages to the experience of Jesus of Nazareth. Christ our suffering Servant knew the abiding strength of the Lord God day after day, insult after insult, injury after injury. Christ does not just ask us to be strong in our own suffering. No, he first suffers—for all humanity—and gives us hope in facing whatever suffering we may bear in our lives.

On this Passion Sunday, we can sharpen not only our understanding of Jesus as the suffering one, but also probe our hearts as we deal with suffering we may be experiencing today. Perhaps a family matter is overwhelming us. Maybe a conflict in the parish is causing great pain. Or a friend or coworker may be undergoing medical treatments that seem to prolong suffering rather than alleviate it.

As we explore suffering, we can forge ahead and keep up our spirits, rejoicing in the mystery of Christ present to us. We can enliven our faith, knowing that not only is there no disgrace in suffering, but there is also the opportunity to testify to others of God's saving care for his people, whatever their circumstance. Remember, God is your help and your salvation—there is no reason to be afraid. God never abandons, never ignores, never repels.

- *Sometimes we may sense that even God is gone from us. That we are alone and without aid; we feel abandoned and, if we are suffering, may feel even more alone. We are, in a word, weary. What word of truth, what word of life might rouse you?*

In this compelling reading Paul challenges us to be as Christ: to have an attitude like his. What might this mean for us?

As you meditate on this poetic reading, note the power that bursts forth from the words before you. We are told of Christ's emptying himself and of his humility. He was obedient beyond measure, to the point of accepting death on the cross.

Jesus is named in this reading as no other can ever be named: Christ. He is the anointed one, the long-awaited Messiah. But he is not only named the Christ; he *is* the Christ. So profound is the reality before us that all the world must assert the joy of the ages: "Jesus Christ is Lord." Our glory is the glory we offer the Father in Christ Jesus. The Holy Spirit gently moves as a satisfying breeze among us to proclaim Christ the Lord in the reality of our moment-to-moment daily living, the framework for our developing spirituality.

Awe and wonder are two words that may express—though incompletely—our response to Jesus humbled and exalted. When we consider his life, his passion, his death and his resurrection, we are probably awestruck at all that he offered for all of humanity. His sacrifice is not only for his disciples. No, his total giving of self is for all people for all time. His sacrifice is both a sign of humility and worthy of the exaltation of God.

Paul tells us that "Christ Jesus, though he was in the form of God/did not regard equality with God/something to be grasped." Think for a moment of how often people today—perhaps even ourselves—may unknowingly seek equality with God by decisions that are made, preferences that are asserted, statements that deny truth and freedom.

Indeed, there are many gods at work today, temporal gods of human creation: selfishgod, propertygod, financialgod, oppressiongod, sportsgod, internetgod. Oh, many more could be named, but the point is clear: the Creator God works through us to overcome inventions of humanity that provide no lasting treasure.

The humbled and exalted One, Jesus Christ, is our model whose attitude must become ours. As we make Christ's attitude our own, we ready ourselves to proclaim the One God and Father of all. We cannot simultaneously adopt this attitude and one or more of the attitudes proposed by the gods mentioned above.

• *Pause and consider a "god" that seeks your praise and time. Then think of one or two concrete ways of maintaining awareness of the living God who promises life, fullness and eternal joy. Be open, once again, to the One for whom we sing in glorious reprise, "Hosanna!"*

Matthew 26:14–27:66

We fidget. We get uncomfortable. We resist being associated with the words we are asked to speak with vigor during the reading of the passion: "Let him be crucified!"

The gospel of Passion Sunday immerses us like no other in the final walk of Jesus. It moves us, ever so slowly, on the way to Calvary, all the while knowing the ending, yet still somehow wanting to change the gospel account—we do not want our Lord to suffer anymore! Please, God, no more.

Jesus is unyielding, however, when it comes to doing the will of God. After celebrating his last meal with his disciples—the Last Supper—he cautions his followers about their faith being put to the test. However, the disciples assure Jesus that their faith would *never* be shaken.

There are many aspects of Matthew's account we could consider here: Jesus' arrest. Jesus before the high priest. Peter's denial. Judas's despair. The dialogue with Pilate. The way of the cross. Jesus' cry, "My God, my God, why have you forsaken me?" His death and giving up of his spirit.

Perhaps we can take a few moments each day this week to

focus on one or more of these powerful dimensions of the passion account. Such reflection can accompany our journey during these solemn days.

For now, consider the experience of Jesus with his tired and sleepy disciples. Nearly brokenhearted from sorrow, he takes three of those closest to him, Peter and Zebedee's two sons, James and John, to Gethsemane. He asks them to keep watch with him while he prays. He experiences "sorrow and distress," and in his prayer affirms that the will of his Father be done.

While Jesus is offering his prayer, his disciples are unable to resist sleep. Understandably tired, they cannot remain alert and awake—watchful with the Lord—as his journey to the cross continues. He exhorts them to stay awake, so that they can keep watch with him. Three times Jesus prays. Each time, the disciples' response is the same: they are unable to "keep their eyes open." Amid Jesus' "sorrow and distress," the disciples rest.

Despite willing spirits, their flesh is weak.

Perhaps we can identify with such a struggle in our own lives. Sometimes we may be willing or intending to do something, yet we are unable to bring it to completion. However, when we are watchful with the Lord, we demonstrate through plentiful and rich lives the holiness of the One who says, "Remain here and keep watch with me." The call to such discipleship is a call to just living, to holiness, to "keeping watch" for the opportunity to assert with renewed and enthusiastic faith the gospel of the Lord.

Such living can be a sign to others of the witness of the gospel, particularly on matters of great importance to the community of faith and of little or no importance to others. Our words, our actions, our inner strivings all need to be intentionally influenced by the church's call to be a people "holy" in the Lord. We can make a difference! We can pursue justice, for example, so that it flows freely and unrestrained in our parishes and our communities.

The call to holiness is rooted in our belief that God alone is holy. Yet God calls each of us to holiness, sharing the divine life of grace with us through the church. This is not a matter of observing that "so-and-so" seems "holier" than another. No, it is much more a matter of searching our hearts for the indwelling Holy Spirit, prompting us to live always as children of God. Such a way of life is a holy way of life, formed as naturally as the aroma of a crockpot slowly and gradually engulfs our home.

We live what we proclaim, ever watchful and ever faithful to Christ Jesus, truly the righteous One. He is God-with-us, holiness personified, justice lived. Let us keep watch, and love as he first loved us.

- *Decision, choice, effort: these and other words can help us focus how we are to live in Christian discipleship. Something more is needed, however, and that is passion. What passion do you bring to your seeking to live a holy life? To live as a person of justice, alert to the presence of the Lord in your midst?*

Renewing Your Life of Faith

Imagine the crowds of people welcoming Jesus into Jerusalem... the throngs of people enthusiastic over his presence...the curiosity seekers, wanting to know what all the fuss is about...the believers, seeking to be near the One from Galilee.

Jesus, who transforms in life and death, is welcomed in a frenzy of excitement. Matthew notes, "The very large crowd spread their cloaks on the road,/while others cut branches from the trees/and strewed them on the road" (21:8). The King had arrived!

On this Sunday, we join the procession of the centuries. Year after year on this day, our community of faith has gathered to sing Hosannas to the Lord of all. We grasp pieces of palm in our hands, extending them forward as they are sprinkled with holy water by the priest. Perhaps the water reminds us of our baptism, that doorway to new life and to the eucharist. We welcome Christ our King, Lord and Messiah of all.

Our welcome and song of praise occur not in Jerusalem, but closer to home, in our local community. How do we welcome Christ today, in this year of Our Lord? What reminders exist for us to praise Jesus in our contemporary society? in our families and homes? at work or at school? What "crowd" to which we belong awaits enthusiastically Christ the redeemer?

We would do well to step back for a moment, exploring how we welcome Christ in our sisters and brothers. Our tradition is rich in works of mercy, so often emphasized during Lenten time. We can renew faith by discerning now how we are messengers of mercy, offering the hand of Christ to the Christ we see in others.

We welcome Christ and offer him praise when we feed the hungry...give drink to the thirsty...clothe the naked...help those imprisoned...shelter the homeless...care for the sick...bury the dead. Our decisions and actions, no matter how simple, reflect our commitment to the Messiah and King whom we honor and praise in the brightness of day and darkening crispness of night.

- *Consider the works of mercy named above. What might you do to ensure that one other person this week knows the mercy and love of Jesus through your hands?*
- *What is your prayer this Passion Sunday? Who needs your prayerful spirit and hopeful attitude right now?*

Accepting the Challenge

Our journey through Lent has taken us to these final days before the Easter triduum. On Holy Thursday the season of Lent will come to an end, and we will enter the most solemn time of the year. Despite the busy-ness of parish preparations for Easter, there is a certain quiet to these last days of Lent, days of heightened reflection and powerful support of our elect and our candidates for Easter sacraments.

During these last Lenten days we remember in prayer each day all who are preparing for Easter sacraments throughout the church. All over the world, groups of people are completing their Lenten time of spiritual preparation, accompanied by parishioners they know well and know not at all. The common support is prayer, invoking the humbled and exalted One to be with them especially in these last days.

One challenge before us—and perhaps more a gentle reminder than challenge—is that of maintaining our growth in the spiritual life after Lent is over. Perhaps these last days of Lent move us to breathe a sign of relief! But do not stop now—the three days of the triduum are nearly upon us, with the Easter season to follow. Our "end" is not Easter, but Christ; our goal is not the completion of Lent, but resting forever in the eternal presence of God.

Christ Jesus, humbled and exalted: may our witness to the Lord be forever on our lips, in our hearts and imbued deeply in our souls. Seek the Lord always, and prepare for the coming of the Lord! May you be ever watchful!

- *Will you take time this week to rest in the Lord? to pause from any usual routine as the church enters the great three days that begin on Holy Thursday?*
- *How might you be even more accepting of the Holy Spirit's moving you to trust, to be merciful, to enter the mysteries we celebrate?*

Prayer for the Week

Lord Jesus Christ,
   you journey to Jerusalem
   and are welcomed in glory and praise.
Later you journey through Jerusalem
   on the way to your death.
Be with us, Lord, as we join your journey
   seek your presence
   rest in you
   and proclaim in mercy and love
   with all our sisters and brothers in faith:
   Humbled One, Exalted One,
   Jesus Christ Is Lord!
                        —*Gerard F. Baumbach*

CHAPTER 7:
SACRED DAYS, LIVES RENEWED

Easter Triduum

Exploring Your Experience

All that we do and all that we are as a community of faith reaches a peak during the sacred days of the triduum—the three days from Holy Thursday evening to Easter Sunday evening. (The liturgical day follows the biblical custom of a day being from evening to evening.) Now, as we celebrate the most solemn time of the entire church year, how do we discern the meaning of the powerful mysteries of faith for our lives?

To be people of faith is to be engaged in a search that can become richer and deeper as life goes on. The Easter triduum is all about the living, the praying and the believing people of faith who see victory in the cross of Christ and rejoicing in the mysteries that give life. Absolutely nothing binds us as people of faith. We are especially aware of this during the sacred triduum when we reassert with compelling vigor our identity as Catholic people.

We may wonder, why do we do this? From the baptismal waters and first sharing of Christ in the eucharist emerge a "walk in newness of life" (*Rite of Christian Initiation of Adults*, #244). But...is this statement intended *only* for those who are, or have been, baptized during the Easter vigil on Holy Saturday night?

Simply put, each of us walks in newness of life as a baptized person of faith. But we do not walk alone, for we are joined with our brothers and sisters on the path of God's people. We are called "the faithful," those already baptized who celebrate the eucharistic sacrifice of Jesus Christ. The fact that we may have been baptized at the age of four weeks, or received first communion when seven years old, does not minimize the importance of our own journey on the walk of new life. In chapter 9 you will be able to explore this theme of new life much more.

The way of Jesus—the way of new life—that directs our living, praying and believing during these three days of the triduum enables us to claim once again our union with Christ our Lord and, through Christ, our sisters and brothers in faith. As you celebrate these three days and continue to nurture the gift of faith, focus on why you choose to live a way of life shaped by the gospel of Jesus, his journey to the cross and his glorious resurrection.

- *What does it mean for you to say:*
  —that you believe in the presence of God in your life?
  —that you believe in Jesus Christ?
  —that you believe in the indwelling Holy Spirit?
  —that you believe in and identify with the church?
  —that you believe in yourself?
- *What good may result from living by what you believe in? Will you try to do this?*

Exploring the Scriptures

Hearing and acting upon the power of the word of God is an essential foundation for our reflection during the triduum.

There is so much proclaimed, we may wonder how we can possibly be attentive to all that we hear. You may find it helpful to select two or three readings for prayer and reflection now, and turn to the others periodically afterward.

The readings of the triduum are listed here to support your reflection, at your own pace, during Holy Week, the Easter season and beyond.

Holy Thursday
Exodus 12:1-8, 11-14
1 Corinthians 11:23-26
John 13:1-15

Good Friday
Isaiah 52:13—53:12
Hebrews 4:14-16; 5:7-9
John 18:1—19:42

Easter Vigil
Genesis 1:1—2:2
Genesis 22:1-18
Exodus 14:15—15:1
Isaiah 54:5-14
Isaiah 55:1-11
Baruch 3:9-15, 32—4:4
Ezekiel 36:16-17a, 18-28
Romans 6:3-11
Matthew 28:1-10

The journey through the word of God that so richly captures the triduum experience is one that sustains and enriches us for much more than three days. Through the retelling of the journey of God's people over the ages and of Christ, Savior and risen One, the Lent-Easter events beckon us to seek the Lord with eager hearts and listening spirits.

The great gospels and other biblical readings of these days move us to that covenant of eternal love given us through the blood of the Lamb of God.

Journey slowly now through this meditation on the word before us, all the while aware of God's call to you. As you read, remember that God loves us unconditionally...and forever.

Refresh your memory with what you hear on Holy Thursday in the Passover account of Moses and the Israelites. Focus on the language describing a lamb, the memorial feast and the call to all generations to "celebrate with pilgrimage to the LORD, as a perpetual institution" (Exodus 12:14).

Consider anew John's gospel account of Jesus' example of service in the washing of the feet of his disciples before the Passover celebration.

Ponder slowly Paul's firm pronouncement to the community at Corinth: "I received from the Lord what I also handed on to you,/that the Lord Jesus, on the night he was handed over,/took bread, and, after he had given thanks,/broke it and said, 'This is my body that is for you./Do this in remembrance of me.'/In the same way also the cup, after supper, saying, 'This cup is the new covenant in my blood./Do this, as often as you drink it, in remembrance of me.'/For as often as you eat this bread and drink the cup,/you proclaim the death of the Lord until he comes." (1 Corinthians 11:23–26).

Remember, too, to open the scriptures to the words of Isaiah proclaimed on Good Friday in which we are reminded of the suffering Servant, the champion of justice, who "grew up like a sapling before him,/like a shoot from the parched earth;/there was in him no stately bearing to make us look at him,/nor appearance that would attract us to him" (Isaiah 53:2).

Recall the great high priest described in the letter to the Hebrews and create your own linkages to the passion account as presented in the gospel of John.

Discover again the wealth of our tradition in the readings of the Easter vigil. Enter into them as you join the journey of faith and life of God's people over the ages. Seek new meanings in new beginnings in the first and second reading from Genesis and enriched understandings from the journey of the Israelites "through the midst of the sea" (Exodus 14:29).

Know the enduring love of your Maker in the fourth reading from Isaiah and refresh yourself with the words of the same prophet in the fifth reading: "All you who are thirsty,/come to the water!" (Isaiah 55:1).

Meditate on the treasures of wisdom from the prophet Baruch: "She [Wisdom] is the book of the precepts of God,/the law that endures forever" (Baruch 4:1).

Seal the experience of the Old yet ever so current Testament with reassuring words from Ezekiel the prophet: "I will give you a new heart and place a new spirit within you" (Ezekiel 36:26).

These seven readings from God's word truly speak of God's

presence, of a journey of faith over the ages, of God's people seeking, moving and responding in faith.

As you focus on the vigil's New Testament proclamations, consider again the words of Paul to the Romans reminding us that our baptism is a baptism into the death and resurrection of Christ: "We were indeed buried with him through baptism into death,/ so that, just as Christ was raised from the dead/by the glory of the Father,/we too might live in newness of life" (Romans 6:4).

A fitting conclusion to this meditation is the proclamation of the gospel from the vigil, in which we hear proclaimed one of the accounts of the women disciples at the tomb of Jesus. For example, Matthew's account tells us they hear of Jesus being raised up and are charged to go and tell the disciples: "He has been raised from the dead,/and he is going before you to Galilee;/there you will see him" (Matthew 28:7). (See also Mark 16:1–7 or Luke 24:1–12.)

However you probe the scriptures during these days, seek first the will of God and his presence to you in symbol, sacrament and one another.

- *What seems to stand out for you from one or more of the readings of the triduum? What impact might your choice have on a decision you will make today or tomorrow? on a relationship that is important to you?*
- *Imagine a person from your community about to be baptized, and hearing the same readings you do. What might the line given above from Ezekiel, about the thirsty coming to the water, mean for this sister or brother of yours? Are you still thirsty for the Lord, even years after your baptism?*

Renewing Your Life of Faith

The Easter triduum ushers in the premier seasonal time to explore and discern with an Easter consciousness the sacraments of initiation: baptism, confirmation and the eucharist. Water, oil, blessings, anointings, candles, garments, signs and actions are not reminders of a distant God, but expressions of the awe-filled presence of God with us.

We gather as the church all over the world on Holy Thursday for the celebration of the eucharist, including the washing of the feet and transfer of the eucharist to a suitable place of repose. On Good Friday we pray the liturgy of the word, venerate the cross and receive Jesus in the communion service (from hosts consecrated on Holy Thursday). No mass is celebrated, however, on Good Friday. On Holy Saturday the church gathers for the great vigil: the service of light, the liturgy of the word, the celebration of baptism and confirmation and the liturgy of the eucharist.

Think now of those coming to the Easter sacraments for the first time. Who has supported their initiation up till now? Who might support them after Easter?

We can become signs to them of what it means to live as disciples of Christ as we unearth the meaning of the mysteries of faith through our own experience of the sacraments during these three days. And we can greet them and rejoice with them after the vigil as well as in the weeks of Easter that follow.

Recall your parish's celebration of the Easter sacraments to help you identify their meaning for you. How did the symbols of the celebration affect you? What mystery did you glimpse through oil, water, bread, wine?

As you continue to renew your life of faith—a renewal made practical by what you face with each new day—remain faithful to Christ who offered himself for all the world. The poem that follows may help you to sharpen your focus as you continue your journey in faith.

The Offering

The offering, of one plus one plus one
    on and on and on
Adding up to more than all of us
Slowly we approach the table
Gathering 'round this bread, this cup
Bless you, Lord,
    for all your creation!
Bless you, Lord,
    for these fruits of our hands!
We present ourselves to you,
    our lives the gifts we share
We place ourselves before you
    sealed in space and time
Where all before meets all that is after
Where all that is under soars beyond all heights
Simple gifts
    our bread, our wine
    blessed, broken
Nourishment
    for the journey from the water
Hope for the unknown day
    breaking forth
    in the freedom of the Spirit
Bonding us, empowering us
God within us
A prayer of life
    and a common sacrifice
    of love poured out
    faith transformed
    hunger satisfied
    thirst quenched
    God among us
    renewing our strength
    to witness in love
    and to come to the altar
    another day.

                —*Gerard F. Baumbach*

- *Is there a line from the poem that might move you toward further reflection? What could it mean for you?*
- *How do your relationships with others affect the way you live your faith?*

Accepting the Challenge

One source for helping us to accept the challenge of living a life of faith professed at baptism is the Easter week sermons of fathers of the church. Speaking in the fourth century, these preachers helped newly baptized members of the church explore the meaning of their baptism in the days following Easter. These fathers would encourage their listeners to reflect on the scriptures and on their experience of the whole baptismal celebration.

One father of the church, John Chrysostom, encouraged newly baptized people this way in the fourth century: "Imitate him [Christ], I beg you, and you will be able to be called newly baptized not only for two, three, ten, or twenty days, but you will be able to deserve this greeting after ten, twenty, or thirty years have passed and, to tell the truth, through your whole life" ("Baptismal Instruction," 5:20).

Each of us must work out for ourselves the best way to live our faith. Whatever we do, we should be mindful of the hope in Christ that joins us together. Paul says in his letter to the Romans: "For in hope we were saved. Now hope that sees for itself is not hope. For who hopes for what one sees? But if we hope for what we do not see, we wait with endurance" (8:24–25).

As you continue to hope with endurance, you may change some attitudes, see things in a new light or decide to reconsider decisions you had made that would "never" be changed. Whatever you do, being patient may help you to discover what makes others think and act as they do when you, perhaps unconsciously, wish they would think and act as you do.

Just as ocean waves that flow randomly or lake breezes that redirect a lake's waters reshape the sands of a shoreline, so too does our parish continue to share in shaping us as disciples of Jesus and members of the church. Oh, we may not glisten as the newly baptized may appear to; however, be assured that we travel with them joyfully on the eucharistic path of assembly prayer, parish identity, mutual support and ongoing formation all life long. Indeed, we are one with them, walking together on the way of mystery and newness of life.

- *Think now of what you believe in, of what you really value about being Catholic. What relationship must you work on as a disciple of Jesus Christ? What decision might you need to make as you uncover new meanings for your life of faith?*
- *Might you be called "newly baptized" now? Why or why not?*

Prayer for the Week

God of mystery,
    be with our parish these three days
    and every day
    as we strive together to
        do your will
        live as disciples of your Son and
        make your name known to all people.
Be with us, Lord, and
    grant that your Spirit will
    move our hearts
    to live for you
    and to know you in the mystery of life
    and eternal embrace of your love. Amen.
                —Gerard F. Baumbach

CHAPTER 8:
AWAKENING FAITH, BEARING WITNESS

Easter Sunday

Exploring Your Experience

Astronauts marvel at planet Earth as they travel through distant, endless skies. Artists try to capture the breadth and movement of the sea in the images they put to canvas. Astronauts, artists, all of us...somehow facing challenges that may propel us to explore new directions!

In this chapter you have the opportunity to explore the challenge of seeking to live as a disciple of the Lord Jesus Christ within the community of faith. Perhaps you will sense a new direction as you discern more about your ongoing conversion in faith—that awakening (or re-awakening) life in Christ.

• *Does this puzzle you? Had you thought that conversion is only for those who were baptized or received into the church during the Easter vigil? What might "ongoing conversion" mean for you?*

One way to discover more about your growth in faith is to go beneath the surface of the obvious meaning of events in your life. Do not dismiss their importance, for *you* are an essential resource for *your* own growth in faith. Indeed, perhaps there are times when you feel cornered or challenged and need to find your way through a difficult situation or strained relationship.

- *Try to think of one example from your life when you felt "cornered." What was it? How did you respond to it? Who supported you?*

We mature and change, move through the hills and valleys and ups and downs of life, and experience a greater sense of where we are headed as we deal creatively with life's challenges. Continue now your own search by discovering through the scriptures more about bearing witness to the Catholic faith you profess and live.

Exploring the Scriptures

The celebration of Easter presents an opportunity to say most positively, "Yes, I believe!" For it is during the liturgy of Easter that we are called to renew the promises of baptism. You are able to affirm your commitment to a Christian way of life. Select one or more of the readings cited here to support your reflection.

The readings for Easter Sunday are:

- *Acts of the Apostles 10:34a, 37–43*
- *Colossians 3:1–4*
- *John 20:1–9*

Acts of the Apostles 10:34a, 37–43

The first reading addresses, in part, being willing to share with others one's experience of and belief in Jesus. The phrase "bear witness" might be used to describe this.

We may bear witness by volunteering our time in a parish human services center. Or we may bear witness by helping young people identify for themselves what they value in life. (Perhaps the challenge of this type of witness is that of support as the young person makes informed personal choices.) As you read this passage, think of ways you can bear witness to your living and, perhaps, awakening faith.

Imagine yourself listening intently to this, Peter's last great discourse, during which he announces the good news of Jesus Christ to the Gentile centurion Cornelius and to Cornelius's family and friends. Peter asserts his faith and that of the other disciples in the risen Christ. He summarizes the account of Jesus' anointing by the Holy Spirit and Jesus' death and resurrection. The message first given to the Jews is now brought to the Gentiles. Awaken, oh, Gentiles!

Peter's words challenge us to believe in Jesus and to reject sin in our lives. For both Jewish Christians and for Gentiles who were soon to be baptized, belief in the risen Christ was of great importance: God granted "that he be visible,/not to all the people, but to us,/...who ate and drank with him after he rose from the dead" (verses 40–41). The author of the Acts of the Apostles goes on to describe the coming of the Holy Spirit upon the Gentiles, before their baptism with water.

- *How do you seek to know God? Are you like Cornelius, still eager to hear about Jesus?*
- *How does Peter's preaching to the Gentiles help you to understand God as a God of all people? How do you feel about that?*

Colossians 3:1-4

The second reading, from Paul, encourages us not to lose sight of Christ as the center of our lives. At work, at home, alone, with others—how you act and your attitude toward life can be influenced by your belief in Jesus the Christ. Paul himself said: "For to me life is Christ, and death is gain" (Philippians 1:21).

Colossians 3:1-4 was written while Paul was under house arrest in Rome, a few years after his third missionary journey. Paul provides a precise guideline for bearing witness: Christ is to be the central point, or turning point, for a Christian, like you, who has died with Christ and risen to new life in the sacrament of baptism.

We Christians are called to accept the transforming power of Christian baptism—certainly, with Christ at its center—and proceed to live the great truths of our faith morning after morning, night after night. At the same time, we must be alert to challenges to our faith. These may be disguised in the false embrace of selfishness, rampant individualism and even unjust nationalism.

- *What might people of faith do to deal constructively with such questions as violence, human rights, economic and ecological issues?*
- *Are there people you know or have heard about who have taken risks in living by their beliefs? Why might they take the risks? What risks might you have to take to live by what you believe?*

John 20:1-9

How does Jesus' resurrection encourage us to live as people who are willing to take risks for what we believe is the right thing to do? This gospel passage challenges us to risk reflecting on the meaning of Jesus' resurrection for our lives.

The time is before dawn on Easter Sunday morning. Mary Magdalene, a disciple of Jesus, observes the empty tomb and alerts Peter and the disciple whom Jesus especially loved. Note how quickly and easily the beloved disciple believed in the risen Jesus. The gospel writer states simply: "[H]e saw and believed." The writer did not demean Peter's faith, but rather elevated the position of the beloved disciple, the one who sat close to Jesus at the Last Supper (John 13:23–25).

In this morning time, this awakening time, the beloved disciple gives an example of one who expresses powerful love unconditionally. The disciple sees the burial cloths in the empty tomb, recognizes that Jesus is risen and comes to a heightened faith in the one he loved and served.

Through the empty tomb, Christians have for centuries "seen" and believed in the risen Christ. By what they have not visibly seen, Christians have, through the gift of faith, believed in Jesus and his raising from death to new life.

This mystery of Jesus' passion, death, resurrection and ascension, called the paschal mystery, is an essential dimension of Catholic belief. Jesus does not only live again, but the offered One is raised from death in a way no person can completely comprehend. Yet by discovering what it means to live as a Christian in the world, one may be able to begin to bear witness to the consequences of the resurrection.

In rising from death, Jesus provides a hope for meeting the challenges that confront us and that can prevent us from becoming our best selves. We Christians are to live in the spirit of the resurrection—with a lively and awakened faith. The challenge here is to see in the uncertainty of life hope for the future. It is a search for life's goodness and for what unites rather than divides, heals rather than hurts and trusts rather than denies.

The challenge we face as Christians is one of confronting and overcoming evil that sometimes may appear to surround us. As Paul points out in his letter to the Ephesians: "For our struggle is not with flesh and blood but with the principalities, with the powers, with the world rulers of this present darkness, with the evil spirits in the heavens" (6:12). Ask yourself:

- *What fears, frights, anxieties or bonds have you or your parish been freed from? Which ones do you or your parish still need to struggle to overcome?*

Renewing Your Life of Faith

Do you recall the scriptures from the first Sunday of Lent? We faced there questions about the evil One, that residue of sinfulness who, given the opportunity, would extinguish your awakening faith. Perhaps you even thought that the theme of evil would be put to rest at the beginning of Lent. After all, isn't that the time to focus on our failings?

Whatever the season, we need to support one another in resisting the ambush of the Tempter. Our walk in the newness of life is not some sheltered pathway to eternity. Rather, it is a lifetime walk of discerning the Holy Spirit in our midst, enabling us by the gift of divine grace to resist whatever might lead us astray—even during Eastertime.

The fathers of the church spoke of a highly symbolic renunciation of sin and profession of faith. For example, Ambrose of Milan reminded the newly baptized: "You renounced the Devil and his works, the world with its luxury and pleasures. Your words are kept not in the tomb of the dead, but in the book of the living" ("The Mysteries," 2:5).

What prevents us from seeking union with Christ and from living no longer as slaves to whatever hinders our movement toward God?

If you go beneath the surface of your thoughts you might discover additional understandings for rejecting evil and the "prince of darkness." Today, people's enslavements may be understood in broader terms. Awareness of local, national and global concerns is a sharp reminder of evil that exists. Look around the block, or around the world through a satellite-fed TV screen, and observe what wrongs need to be righted, what sinful attitudes might be corrected. What a challenge!

Evil remains in many ways a mystery of its own that cannot be addressed only by social programs and projects. Still, in acting to overcome evils you may be aware of, you enter your name in the "book of the living" and commit yourself to the work of the Prince of peace.

- *What might you need to do to sever any bonds that might impede your committing yourself to Christ?*
- *Do you see evils where you live that need to be overcome? If so, what might you do to help?*

Accepting the Challenge

Enter now more deeply into the mystery of your own baptism. Explore for a few moments what leads you to profess your faith.

Perhaps there are levels of understanding you have reached that would move you beyond the meanings you see here. For example, you may have a new insight into some specific difficulties you face daily. You may want to take a new look at one or more relationships in your life. Or you may be struggling with a moral issue, and something in this chapter may have triggered some new alternatives for you. In short, you may be discerning the prompting of the Holy Spirit, awakening you to walk confidently with your parish in the newness of life.

Perhaps you will come to see that a most appropriate baptismal symbol—even if you were baptized as an infant—is your life as a person of faith. This active faith now calls you to do what you can to render justice where necessary, correction when called upon and love for all.

The consequences of your baptism are, in a sense, what you make of them. Continue to grow into your baptism as you discover more along your journey of faith. Baptized in water and the Spirit, you are challenged to risk—yes, risk—continuing to live out your baptism. You are challenged to risk professing your faith and to risk rejecting whatever would prevent you from becoming or remaining a person of justice and peace. The risk is one taken not alone, but with other disciples— whether baptized ten days, twenty months or thirty years ago.

The central question to ask yourself now is: What meaning does all this have to do with your life? What does your profession of faith have to do with challenges you are facing right now?

By sharpening your awareness of your whole attitude toward God and others, the faith of the church can become more thoroughly your own. Imagine yourself as one just emerging from the waters of baptism—delightfully cleansed and refreshed and renewed in spirit!

- *How can you try to be a "beloved disciple"?*
- *What can you do to profess your faith in word and action? In other words, how might you continue to affirm your faith in one specific way? How might your parish?*

Remember these words of Paul: "...I consider life of no importance to me, if only I may finish my course and the ministry that I received from the Lord Jesus, to bear witness to the gospel of God's grace" (Acts 20:24). In an attitude of faith and trust, recall your ongoing conversion to Christ. Be awake and bear witness.

Prayer for the Week

Marvelous and mysterious God,
　　you welcome us...
　　you free us...
　　you penetrate our lives
　　　　with the gift of your Son.
Awaken us to risk
　　reaching beyond our boundaries
　　to invite others
　　to come to know you
　　in word and sacrament.
Be with us always
as we profess our faith in you,
　　bearing glorious witness to your Holy Name,
　　now and forever. Amen.
　　　　　　　　　　　　—Gerard F. Baumbach

CHAPTER 9:
NEW LIFE, DAILY LIFE

Second Sunday of Easter

Exploring Your Experience

Water, water everywhere...perhaps the usual refrain of people
who are baptized as adults into the Catholic Church. For most
of us, however, baptism came when we were infants, so there
are no personal memories of immersion or of having the water
poured over our heads three times. In fact, many of us probably do not know (without checking!) the date of our baptism.

It is not too late for you, if you were baptized as an infant
or even as an adult, to discover anew the experience of initiation into the church. Whether you were baptized as an infant
or as an adult, the church did not quickly "towel-dry" you
after baptism, hoping to prepare you for casting as from a
preformed baptismal mold or restore you to a former self. No,
even though it may have appeared that people assisting may
have been ready with their towels, the waters of rebirth
remain, soaking into every pore of your being, claiming you
for Christ.

Water in all its power can be beautiful, serene and life-sav-
ing. Read the following poem slowly and thoughtfully.

> *Baptism*
> Water, flowing quickly
> Streams of wonder I behold.

Yet how gently strength arises
And gives to me a hundredfold.

O, these fountains of joy unending
O, these brooks of lasting peace!
Silent, flowing, gently easing,
Carve into my life, appeasing.

Winds its way through many caverns
Bubbling, churning,
Filling, swelling,
Wonderful, compelling.

Cool and clear, I drink with delight
For the rays of day break forth
How I feel how much I'm loving
All the joys of my new birth.
　　　　　　　—Elaine Holena-Baumbach

- *Is there a line in the poem that appeals to you differently from the others? What connections triggered your choice?*
- *Try to identify an example of the beauty or power of water from your life. Why would you select this example?*
- *Imagine yourself entering the baptismal waters. The deacon or priest is about to immerse you, not once, but three times. What might this image tell you about new life? About the primary symbol of baptism?*

Exploring the Scriptures

The phrase *new life* describes well the life shared by the early Christian community. Reflect on what new life is for you as you pray the scriptures cited here, and as you continue to live as a faithful member of your parish.

The readings for the second Sunday of Easter are:

- *Acts of the Apostles 2:42–47*
- *1 Peter 1:3–9*
- *John 20:19–31*

Acts of the Apostles 2:42–47

This classic reading invites us to discover how the early Christians changed their ways of living. The first-century group of believers in Jesus saw their fellowship together as a way of life. The first verse of the passage identifies their activities as four in number: concern for the apostles' teaching; sharing life together in a spirit of fellowship; taking meals together; and sharing prayer. Their religious identity was not something separate from their way of life. It was at the heart of who they were.

What example might we derive from these early disciples? For one thing, we might pray together in our homes. Not an earth-shattering and terribly creative idea, but an altogether essential one. When these early believers broke bread in their homes, this was not just a coming together to eat at the appointed time. This everyday experience had a religious meaning.

Throughout the world and in scripture itself, bread is the source of maintaining health and life. Bread was used by Jesus as a powerful sign of his continuing union with his disciples. But this is no ordinary sign. The bread and wine become Jesus' body and blood, to be given always to his disciples. In baptism, water is the sign of new life. But it is a powerful sign— it actually brings about what it signifies: new life, God's life!

During the Easter season, you join with other parishioners and enter into the mystery of Christ present in the eucharist. You do not simply extend hand or tongue in some routine motion. Rather, you take the gift of the Father, given in unconditional and abiding love. The question that remains is, how do you share the new life that is yours as a child of God? Some ways one might share with others are by checking in with a neighbor who is housebound; assisting in a parish food drive; or encouraging catechumens who are now preparing for baptism.

- *Why do you think the early disciples acted as they did? What do you think motivates you and your parish to act in abiding love?*

1 Peter 1:3–9

The second reading, from Peter's letter to Gentile Christians in Asia Minor, explores the new birth given by Jesus Christ. This new birth is a birth "to a living hope" (1 Peter 1:3): what an encouraging statement for us.

The passage is from a letter written as encouragement to Christians undergoing suffering at the hands of nonbelieving neighbors in Asia Minor. Peter urges them to "stand fast" for what they believe in and reminds them of the focus of their life of faith—the risen Christ.

Jesus is the hope for the Christian, for those who are suffering and in distress. The cause for rejoicing for Christians is an attitude of hope that can become a source of great joy.

Are there challenges in your life that make it difficult for you to live as a person of hope? Perhaps you are facing a "dead-end" situation at work, a friendship may be under strain or you may be at odds with a neighbor. It may seem like "new life" escapes you.

- *How do you feel about this situation? Can you do anything about it? How?*

Pray, right now, for the calm and help of the Holy Spirit and those who are close to you to face this situation openly and with a renewed sense of hope. Remember that your parish community is called to be one with you in prayer and in spirit. This is the community that prays in hope for your ongoing conversion to Christ and constant witness to your life in Christ. Invite others to pray with you, too.

John 20:19–31

The gospel for the second Sunday of Easter tells of Jesus' appearance to the disciples after the resurrection.

The disciples of Jesus are huddled together on the evening of Easter, fearful after Jesus' death on the cross. Jesus comes to them, however, offers them peace and then offers it again. This peace is no ordinary greeting—a first-century substitute for "Hello, there." Rather it is an expression of what Jesus himself brings to his disciples: loving concern, calm, lack of fear...in a word, peace.

Jesus breathes on his disciples and offers the gift of the Holy Spirit and power to forgive sin. The breathing of Jesus is no accident—he could have just as easily used words alone or even presumed the disciples' willingness to do as he asked. In the word *breathe,* one may really see echoes of the creation of humanity in Genesis 2:7: "[T]he LORD God formed man out of the clay of the ground and blew into his nostrils the breath of life, and so man became a living being."

You may also see here a reminder of what was said about the breath of the Spirit in chapter 1 of this book. Jesus offers us, too, the Holy Spirit—breath of life and gift of the risen Lord.

- *Become more aware now of the refreshing breath of life that is yours. Sit in a comfortable chair, and let all your muscles relax. Feel the relaxation from head to toe. Now take a deep breath, all the way in. Slowly exhale. Then repeat the breathing exercise. Know that the Holy Spirit gives life to your soul, power to your being and seeks to reside always in your heart.*

Renewing Your Life of Faith

The gospel passage for this Sunday describes the absence of Thomas the apostle from the appearance of Jesus on Easter night. One really has to feel sympathy for Thomas. In a way he represents the doubt of all of the disciples regarding Jesus' resurrection. But, as the passage of time and the concreteness of history would have it, only Thomas is named as doubting the Easter event. Poor Thomas!

Thomas's attitude is one of unbelief until it can be proven to him that Jesus is truly risen. He refuses to accept even the evidence offered by his friends ("We have seen the Lord!"). He persists in his attitude of wanting only to see for himself, as if to say, "Hey, I want to see this miracle, too!" How sad for Thomas that he would not—or could not—trust his friends. But what a turnaround occurs when he casts his eyes on Jesus! Without even touching the risen One, Thomas firmly declares, "My Lord and my God!"

The last part of the passage shows the purpose of John's gospel: to help believers deepen their faith in Jesus as the Messiah and Son of God. Through faith in Jesus, the believer is called to new life. The source of this new life is Jesus himself. What is necessary is not seeing, but believing in Jesus as the Christ, the Son of God. Daily we decide to renew our life in faith.

- *What role do you think "hearing" plays in faith? "Seeing"?*
- *Is it sometimes difficult for you to place your trust in God? If so, why?*

Although you may sometimes think of baptism only as a specific moment in time (for example, "when I was baptized"), it is part of what one experiences during initiation into the church. Perhaps one could describe living one's baptism as a journey over time to saying "yes" to a lifestyle founded on the divine life, the life of sanctifying grace given in baptism.

Your participation in the life of the church empowers you to explore what it means to believe and to live as a Christian. You may discover how much you rely on others to help you do this as you continue your journey of faith in the midst of your parish. The renewal of baptismal promises is one way to affirm this.

Discover more now of what the celebration of baptism means for you. In the early church it was customary for people to be baptized by immersion. Later on, pouring water over the candidate, who was standing in a pool, became a popular practice. Today, baptismal practice varies within the Catholic Church.

In chapter 2, we reflected on your call to live a holy life as a blessing of God. Recall that in baptism, you entered into the paschal mystery of Christ by sharing in his death and resurrection. Indeed, the water used for your baptism was blessed as part of the celebration of the sacrament. How richly blessed are the people of God!

Your baptism was one in a long line of baptismal celebrations over the ages. Christian baptism is rooted in the scriptures and is part of a long tradition. As you saw in chapter 7, the fathers of the church, speaking in the fourth century, explored the baptism celebration with the newly baptized in descriptive and symbolic language.

Two basic themes dominate the fathers' preaching on baptism: union with Christ in his death and resurrection and the whole idea of new birth, or new life in Christ. Theodore of Mopsuestia compared the water to a womb that protects the person who is being baptized. Just as the conceived child has lived in the shelter and security of its mother's womb, so, too, does the candidate for baptism experience, in a symbolic way, the womblike protection of the water. The newly baptized emerges from the waterlike womb born anew to live as a Christian.

As you live the new life of baptism in your daily life, consider how such living challenges you. How might you respond to this example?

- *City planners decide to replace an unattractive downtown urban neighborhood with a futuristic mall designed to include exclusive boutiques and high-priced apartments. The decision will result in displacing hundreds of low-income families. Where do you stand on this situation? What might a parish do to help local residents? What could "resurrection" mean to them?*

Accepting the Challenge

What is the daily challenge of "new life" for you as a Christian? You may hear homilies on living as a committed Christian, as a person baptized in water and the Holy Spirit. Yet this new life is not intended to separate you from problems you may have. Rather, it is intended to be a source of strength to help you live each day in a spirit of trust and hope. You can become a "realistic optimist"—looking forward to the fullness of life with God while at the same time trying to cope with the tensions of life today.

The questions that follow may help you to focus on your attitude as a Christian. They may challenge you to rethink decisions you have made or judgments you have formed.

- *What responsibility do you have toward making newcomers feel welcome in your parish, neighborhood or town?*
- *Should you work on or change any of your attitudes toward others because of the way you have judged a situation or another person? How might you be "new life" to another?*

Do you have a candle from your baptism? even from years ago? Take your candle, or a new baptismal candle, and feel the smooth texture of the wax as you look at the symbols impressed on the candle.

At your baptism, a godparent received a lighted candle from the presider. It was lighted from the Easter candle and signified your sharing in the life of Christ, who is our light. Jesus said, "I am the light of the world. Whoever follows me will not walk in darkness, but will have the light of life" (John 8:12).

Light the candle. Focus on the symbols that identify Jesus Christ as the beginning (A) and the end (Ω) and that indicate the first two letters of the sacred name Christ in Greek (X and P). Notice, too, the symbol of the dove—a symbol of the peace and gift of the Holy Spirit that is yours. Put the candle on a table or countertop in front of you. Watch it burn momentarily. Before extinguishing it, pray the prayer for the week that follows.

Prayer for the Week

Gracious and loving God,
each person I meet is a living reminder of
    your welcome to me in the saving gift of baptism.
You rescue me from all that would harm me
and sustain me with the fire of your love each day.
Through your Son, Jesus Christ, my daily life is new life.
Through the power of your Spirit,
    the warmth of new life burns without ceasing in my heart.
Be with me, Lord, as I bear the fire of your love to all around
        me
    and enable me to proclaim the wonder of your eternal
        embrace
    to the stranger, the meek one, the powerful one, the lonely
        one,
    and all who hunger for the new life only you can give.
Praise you, Lord, for immersing me in the fire of your love.
    Amen.

                                        —Gerard F. Baumbach

CHAPTER 10:
HOPE NOURISHED, HUNGER SATISFIED

Third Sunday of Easter

Exploring Your Experience

On the night of the Easter vigil, your parish invited those who had just been baptized and received into the church to the table of the eucharist for the first time. It is likely, however, that all present hungered for eucharist. Recall the words of Paul to the Corinthians: "Because the loaf of bread is one, we, though many, are one body, for we all partake of the one loaf" (1 Corinthians 10:17). We come to the altar from which we draw nourishment for life, ready to share in the one loaf.

We really never stop preparing for eucharist. Our preparation is part of our conversion to Christ and ongoing growth in the Christian life.

Your conversion may be gradual, slowly winding its way over the rough and smooth edges of your life. Along the way you may feel the joy of new relationships with others...trust that others will be with you...doubt about what you are doing...a warm embrace when words won't do...loneliness when you feel misunderstood...a burning love for Jesus...sadness when someone moves away...the Holy Spirit speaking in your heart...a wonderful new experience of hospitality.

For a Catholic, like you, the eucharist can become the center of your hope. The eucharist can become not only what we hunger for ourselves, but what we strive to share with others. When you see a need in someone else's life and try to help, then you are living the eucharist. When you voice your concern about an important issue, then you are living the eucharist. The way you choose to live can be an example of the central place of the eucharist in your life.

- *How can prayer and action become an even larger part of a single fabric of faith for you?*

Exploring the Scriptures

Our hunger for eucharist is linked to our hunger for the word of God. You may want to ponder this thought as you explore today's readings.

The readings for the third Sunday of Easter are:

- *Acts of the Apostles 2:14, 22–33*
- *1 Peter 1:17–21*
- *Luke 24:13–35*

As you reflect on the readings, try to focus on what your sharing in the eucharist, the bread of life, means to you as spiritual nourishment for your faith journey. Perhaps this will lead you to explore what you and your parish are called to be for others.

Acts of the Apostles 2:14, 22–33

In this reading, Peter boldly announces this essential truth: that God freed Jesus from death and raised him up.

In chapter 8, you were encouraged to read Peter's last great discourse. This reading is his first. The scene for this passage is Pentecost Sunday. The disciples are gathered together in Jerusalem and are "filled with the holy Spirit" (Acts 2:4). They boldly begin to speak of "the mighty acts of God" (Acts 2:11) and are even accused by some of speaking like drunkards. Peter, however, rises and begins his sermon. One can imagine the fiery and compulsive Peter jumping to his feet!

Peter tries to show that Jesus is the Promised One, the Messiah. The cross could not hold Jesus captive: "[I]t was impossible for him to be held by it [death]" (Acts 2:24). In rising from death, Jesus provides hope for meeting whatever challenges us.

Consider the dyings and risings people experience today. Perhaps someone you know has suffered a serious setback in business, while another has just healed a broken friendship. A mother may gaze lovingly at a photograph of her missing child on a milk carton, wondering if they will ever be united again. A teenager may overcome drug dependency after a struggle that had once seemed futile.

The deaths people experience today may not steal a last breath, but may provide a clue as to what must be done to overcome sin and injustice. By resisting quick judgments people begin to overcome evil that might otherwise overtake them.

• *What "deaths" seem to challenge you repeatedly? How might you deal with them in light of this reading? Might a member of your parish be a source of hope and support for you as you try?*

1 Peter 1:17–21

This passage is very brief—only five verses long. Peter does not beg or meekly ask the baptized to believe what he says. In this and surrounding passages, he urges the baptized to remain faithful to God, for they are made new by Christ. He reminds them that they are delivered "by Christ's blood beyond all price." Indeed, Jesus sacrificed himself for all. He surrendered, sacrificed, yielded all for all humanity.

This blood image is a very powerful one. The blood of the lamb was sprinkled on the lintel and doorposts of the homes of the Israelites to protect them from being struck down as the Egyptians were (Exodus 12:21–30). In Israelite law, the use of blood, symbolic of life itself, was particularly important in sacrificial rites of forgiveness (Leviticus 17:1–16).

Moses, in ratifying the Sinai covenant, splashed blood on the altar and sprinkled it on the people, saying, "This is the blood of the covenant which the LORD has made with you in accordance with all these words of his" (Exodus 24:8). During the Passover meal, Jesus took a cup of wine, gave thanks and passed it to his disciples. "He said to them: 'This is my blood of the covenant, which will be shed for many'" (Mark 14:24).

Jesus' sacrifice for all—the shedding of his blood, the giving of his life—is the sacrifice in which we share today, the sacrifice of the mass. Your hunger for Christ in the eucharist is not your hunger alone. Such hunger pains are not limited only to each person individually. Rather, we hunger as a community of faith, yearning for the body and blood of the risen One, surrendering our lives to him and one another as we await the eternal celebration of life everlasting. Can we do any less out of love for the One who sacrificed himself for all humanity?

How, then, does Jesus' death and resurrection have an impact on how you live your life today? Surely Peter did not intend to provide only an explanation of past events to the baptized. His purpose was to move his readers to action, to see these events as somehow present in their own lives. Such is the case with us today as well.

A Christian is joined to Christ in the eucharist and shares in Jesus' dying and rising. Christians are called to share the eucharist, resulting in their giving of themselves as people nourished by the blood of the Lamb, Jesus Christ, the One who redeemed the world.

- *Look around your neighborhood or town. What evidence is there of Christians living by what they believe?*

Luke 24:13–35

Recall a memorable journey. Were you alone? With a companion? Why did you go?

The journey to Emmaus, reported in today's gospel, surely was a memorable journey. What a walk! Seven miles—a long journey by foot. The travelers, two disciples of Jesus who had hoped he was the Messiah, are ready to go home from Jerusalem. After being there for the events surrounding the Passover and Jesus' death, they set out, discussing as they go all that had happened during the last few days.

An inquiring stranger comes by and joins them. The trio walk and talk for hours. This leads the two who had begun the journey to wonder about their mysterious companion. Perhaps they thought, "He knows so much about the scriptures, yet he does not know what happened in Jerusalem?"

The wonder of the travelers does not lead them to part from the stranger; rather, their curiosity and puzzlement move them to invite him to stay with them. Before long, they are sharing a meal. Though it is not his home, the stranger plays host, serving the two travelers bread blessed and broken. In the breaking of bread, their eyes are opened—aware now of the presence of their Lord in their midst—and the traveler-host vanishes. However, they feel no absence. Strange, isn't it? In the absence of the stranger they are conscious of the presence of the Messiah.

Nourished by the word of God on their way to Emmaus, the travelers share the bread that was broken and given to them by the one whose presence they had hungered for. Despite the growing darkness, they hurry back to Jerusalem and tell the story of coming to know the stranger in the breaking of the bread.

There are interesting parallels to the celebration of the eucharist here. Jesus explains the scriptures to the two disciples, and the action of sharing the bread resembles what Jesus did at the Passover meal: "Then he took the bread, said the blessing, broke it, and gave it to them..." (Luke 22:19).

One might imagine Jesus gathering annually with other faithful Jews to recall the great Exodus experience of Passover. Perhaps their feelings were of entering into the Passover event itself—of somehow knowing a freedom from bondage that could not be duplicated. It is from within this sacred setting—that of a meal—that Jesus came to us under the appearances of bread and wine.

You have a story to tell, just as the travelers did who risked the return trip to Jerusalem. But you are not dealing with a stranger. No, Jesus travels with you as you face the risks of life at the turn of the millennium. The Son of God is with you, beckoning you to himself through the witness and ministry of his church. What hope does this offer you? What meaning?

It means becoming aware of the eucharist as a sacrament of our union with one another as the body of Christ, the church. This union is brought about by the loving action of the Holy Spirit.

It means taking a closer look at the virtue of hope in your life.

It means clarifying how Jesus is the center of your life of faith.

It means exploring how Jesus makes a difference in your attitudes and in how you relate to people who are close to you—and those who are not.

The travelers in the story did not recognize the stranger on the way to Emmaus. Was there a time recently when you did not see what was right before you; when you couldn't see the forest for the trees? What did you do?

• How welcome might a stranger feel in your parish? Why? Will you try to ensure that there is a spirit of hospitality?

Renewing Your Life of Faith

The celebration of eucharist is also a time to affirm what you believe in the profession of faith, already offered for your reflection in chapter 3. The eucharist moves you beyond time to a timeless expression of your relationship with God and of the blending of your life with the lives of other parishioners. Together you give thanks. And together you are called to be present in all your senses—smell, touch, sight, hearing, taste and in the depths of your heart. Then, as the liturgy unfolds, you may reaffirm your belief in God as the center of your life of faith, the One for whom Christians hunger.

Yet how can one speak to a person about spiritual matters when one's stomach aches and one's mouth is dry? The need for food is people's most basic physical need. Perhaps what needs to be emphasized is the connection between physical and spiritual hungers.

For us, this link is the experience of the liturgy of the mass. Perhaps you may see this experience as being called not only to worship God with others, but also to go forth from this mystery to live justly in your everyday life. By thinking this way, you may be better able to identify with those who are without food. You may be able to begin to feel their basic needs, and they may begin to be able to feel yours.

What might this mean? It could mean that you may end up revealing hungers in your life. These hungers may have nothing to do with calories and carbohydrates, but with other basics, like spiritual growth and inner peace. Indeed, persons who are physically starving or malnourished may be able to help you discover the living bread. Recall the words of Jesus: "I myself am the living bread that came down from heaven; whoever eats this bread will live forever; and the bread that I will give is my flesh for the life of the world" (John 6:51). We are privileged to partake of the Bread of Life—of Christ with us—in the eucharistic celebration, the mass.

Another way to understand hunger is to view it as the deepest longing of a person. You might say that this greatest hunger lies at the very center of who you are. As you look back on your life, you may uncover what it is that makes you who you are. This does not mean only trying to recall as much as you can of your past. That is part of life's journey, but not all of it. The past of your life is not behind you, but under you. It supports you and is part of your search, your journey of faith.

This search for what lies at the center of your life may have started years ago. Or you may be beginning now to discover what you hunger for. It is never too late. This search may also be a painful one. Why do people struggle with life's most basic questions? Why do people take years to find their niche in a chosen career or job? Why do college students change majors? Why do people decide to join one organization over another? Or leave one for another?

The pain involved in seeking what you hunger for may sometimes appear to be more than you can bear. However, the hope you carry within the recesses of your soul and the help you gain from relationships with others may provide strong support as you search for what is at the center of your life. As you journey, you may begin to understand better hungers in your life, what you yearn for and will not live without.

• *What does it mean for you to seek God? How can you relate your sharing in eucharist with your parish to the practical realities and problems you face every day?*

Imagine hungers in your life. Pursue how you relieve them. Try to discover what you might do to relieve others' hungers as well. Then, during the next few days, discuss with one or two other people the last line of today's second reading: "Your faith and hope, then, are centered in God."

Accepting the Challenge

"[W]ho knows what pertains to a person except the spirit of the person that is within" (1 Corinthians 2:11)? Who knows for sure what lies at the depths of who you are?

Identifying your greatest hunger may help to clarify your ongoing conversion to Christ. It may also lead you beyond your own needs, to look at needs that may exist around you. For example, a catechumen in your parish may be in need of a sponsor. Will you offer to walk the way of life in Christ with this person?

• One question for you to think about now is: How can the presence of Jesus to you in the eucharist help you as you try to live as a person of compassion, justice and mercy?

The strength or weakness of your relationships to others will not just change overnight. Hopefully, however, there is a foundation of support in your parish that can help you to become better informed about what makes your parish tick and what are its vital concerns. In other words, to help you see what is at the center of parish life, to help you see that for which your parish hungers.

As you live your faith each day, you become even more a part of the fiber of a community of people who share a story of faith of which your own story is part. You are invited to continue that story by gathering with others to come to the altar for the nourishment of the eucharist. Yes, the eucharist: more than our nourishment for one hour a week, the eucharist—the center of our life of faith—is the parish's nourishment for the whole week.

Prayer for the Week

Lord of the journey of life,
    you nourish us with the gift of your Son,
    the One whom we seek,
    the One for whom we long,
    the One who redeems us
and who is present in the eucharist.
Be with us, Lord,
    and take our yearning
    our thirst
    our hunger
    our hope
and transform us into a people blessed
    with the power of your Word,
    with lives centered on you,
    God and Father of all,
    in the Holy Spirit, now and forever. Amen.
                    —Gerard F. Baumbach

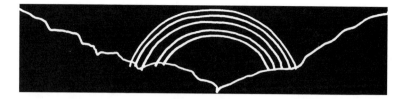

CHAPTER 11:
REAL LONGING, FULL AND ABUNDANT LIFE

Fourth Sunday of Easter

Exploring Your Experience

Fullness or abundance of life: What is it? What do we long for in life?

For a child it may be the first time riding on a bicycle, or being welcomed into the neighborhood group as a "regular."

For a young adult it may be making it to the championship round with an underdog team.

The personals column of the classified section of a newspaper gives a glimpse of what adults may long for:

Sam, Thank you for coming back to me. I need you and love you. Love, Marianne.

Amy, I have always loved you and always will. You are life to me. I will return to you someday and will never leave you or the kids again. Please contact me.

For others fullness of life may be the dream of a new start in a new land, a new beginning following bankruptcy proceedings or a feeling of exhilaration after a medical lab test comes back negative.

Even with suggestions from other people's experiences, it may be difficult to determine what fullness or abundance of life may mean for you today. Advertisers promote all kinds of products that promise fulfillment or success. People struggle mercilessly to reach personal goals and, when they finally do, are sometimes disappointed. One can almost hear them asking, Is that all there is?

For some Christians, fullness of life may be directly related to a blossoming prayer life. One may participate in a prayer group or parish devotions or develop a personal prayer style that is particularly fulfilling. One may express thanks and praise to God in the gathering with others for eucharist.

Fullness of life may be a high point in your life. It may be an ongoing sense of coming to know more about Jesus, yourself and how you relate to others. It may be no more than saying "Aha!" to some new insight or some hidden indescribable meaning associated with an experience you've had. However you may describe fullness of life now, this chapter may help you discover what you continue to long for and what this life in abundance can be for you as you live in Christian discipleship.

• *If you were asked to explain the fullness of life to another person, what might you say?*

Exploring the Scriptures

The challenges we face—sometimes even daily—can make us feel like we are in a mental tug of war about living for the fullness of life. What are we to do? Probing the word of God in the scriptures can yield heightened awareness of that for which we long. We can remind ourselves of these words of Jesus from today's gospel: "I came so that they might have life and have it more abundantly" (John 10:10).

As you reflect on the scriptures identified below, recall what prompts you to live and act as a Christian, to live for the abundant gift of life in Christ.

The readings for the fourth Sunday of Easter are:

- *Acts of the Apostles 2:14a, 36–41*
- *1 Peter 2:20b–25*
- *John 10:1–10*

Acts of the Apostles 2:14a, 36–41

Imagine how much has been written and said over two thousand years in the name of Jesus Christ! Some might say that no other name is used so frequently for such a wide variety of purposes: for example, in prayer, in anger, in teaching. In its most basic meaning, Jesus means "God saves," and Christ, "the anointed one." As you read the passage, think of what you mean when you say the name of our Lord and Savior, Jesus Christ.

The reading includes another part of Peter's address on Pentecost (chapter 10 included an earlier part). Here Peter asserts that his audience must reform and be baptized in the name of Jesus Christ. The passage presents the pattern of Christian initiation in the New Testament: evangelization of the inquirers, leading to conversion and baptism.

Peter's call to reform one's life and to be baptized is linked to the forgiveness of sins. This repentance is to be taken as a change of heart, a turning to Jesus, whom "God has made both Lord and Christ." Peter also associates the gift of the Holy Spirit with the individual's baptism. The Holy Spirit, given in baptism, was indeed promised by the risen Christ (Acts 2:33). Luke, author of the Acts of the Apostles, notes in the gospel also attributed to him that Jesus returned from his baptism in the Jordan River "[f]illed with the holy Spirit" (4:1). The Holy Spirit was a source of strength and power for Jesus.

Perhaps you may want to recall now the strength and power of the Holy Spirit in your life. Your daily turning to Jesus may be understood as a gradual awareness of the presence of God, prompting you to seek, investigate, learn about and discover the life of grace that is yours, given in baptism. The new life that directs our walk in faith fosters our living for the fullness of life. Pause now and ponder the following:

- *Who, for you, is an example of the power and wonder of God? What does this person bring out in you?*

1 Peter 2:20b–25

This reading is directed to workers who often served under severe masters. Peter does not address the social evil of slavery, but discusses the manner in which the follower of Christ is called to accept suffering at the hands of unjust people. The model for such a worker is Jesus, the suffering Servant.

Frequently situations of suffering are "settled" by violent means. Police may storm an apartment house when a family member threatens others because he or she can't take the pressure of family life anymore. Oppressed people around the world struggle for peaceful solutions, but often violence erupts. The suffering of a strained relationship between a couple may result in abuse or verbal threats.

Peter rejects all violence, even when it might be justified in the opinion of the oppressed. He urges his readers to remember that Christ suffered for all, doing so willingly on the cross. By Christ's wounds, we are made whole. Through Christ's death, we are reconciled with God. In him we find that for which we long. Jesus is the way to life with God that is beyond any ending in time.

Explore further who Christ is and what he means for your life. The challenge is to live in discipleship with others as members of the church, doing the best you can with your own abilities, keenly aware of the presence of God in your waking and sleeping, working and resting, praying and playing. This means coming to know more about who you are, what you are about. It means, really, trying to discover ever so gently Christ's continuing presence in your life as you follow his example. You may want to complete one or more of the following to help you focus on Jesus' presence in your life.

- *The next time you visit a mall or shopping center, observe the expressions on the faces of people as they go about their business. Do you see suffering in their faces? Hope? What else might you see? Why?*
- *Some people may comment this way about suffering: "Why does God allow it?" "Suffering can make you strong." "People bring it on themselves." Despite such observations, the most difficult suffering to deal with may be one's own. Are you suffering now? If you are, what support might you need?*
- *Ponder this question: What value might there be in suffering "with" another person?*

John 10:1–10

This passage comes just before the well-known words of Jesus, "I am the good shepherd" (verse 11). The images of shepherd and gate for the sheepfold were common to the people of Jesus' time, and it was not so unusual for Jesus to talk about them. Although these images are not so immediately present to us, the power of the story is just as valid today. As you read this passage, try to recall what motivates you to place your faith in Jesus.

Jesus' words are addressed to some Pharisees who were not seeing eye to eye with him. In this passage the leaders are compared to thieves who refuse to enter the fold through the gate.

Jesus' words, however, can be addressed to all people and not just to the audience John the evangelist chose to write about.

As we see, Jesus is not only a shepherd here, but the gate to the sheepfold as well. He not only leads his followers to fullness of life, but that life can be found in him. The one who responds to Jesus the shepherd will "find pasture": sharing in the life of God.

One informative aspect of this parable is the sense of intimacy and care that the shepherd has for his sheep. The response of the sheep to the shepherd is not automatic; they must first hear his voice. One might suggest that a special bond exists between shepherd and sheep. How familiar are you with the voice of your shepherd? What voice do you hear?

Today, one may feel pressure to listen to many different voices. For example, newspaper headlines may tell us:

FUROR SURROUNDS TEEN COUNSELING CLINIC
ELDERLY COUPLE BEGS DOCTOR: LET US DIE
AIDS CHILDREN: SCHOOL CONTROVERSY WIDENS

These examples merely suggest some voices we may hear as we try to live as people of faith. Other voices may be closer to home. For example, you may be torn between the opinions of a friend and a spouse on how to resolve a long-standing conflict with a neighbor. You may be struggling to get close to a lonely relative, to really understand, to listen as attentively as you can. But you sense nothing happens. You may feel that you're at a dead end. What do you do?

Consider for a moment some voices Jesus heard. It may be easy sometimes to forget that Jesus did not always have a receptive audience. He was rejected, not once but twice in his home-town of Nazareth (John 4:43–54; Mark 6:1–6); was persecuted for curing a man on the sabbath (John 5:1–18); and was scolded for forgiving the sins of the paralytic (Luke 5:17–26).

Some of us may think, "If only I were more like Jesus, I'd be able to...." The challenge is to accept Jesus of Nazareth as the one who calls you to hope in the future—indeed, a timeless future—as you face the practical circumstances of everyday life. It is in Jesus that we find abundance of life. It is the voice of the risen One that calls you to fullness of life.

- *Imagine yourself at a parish meeting. Many "voices" are having their say. The person leading the meeting thanks you for coming and expresses hope that you will participate as the meeting proceeds. How do you feel about speaking up?*
- *What could you do to help a person you know who may be experiencing a difficult personal situation?*

Renewing Your Life of Faith

One of our principal beliefs is that of the presence of the risen Christ in the church. The Christian community frequently has looked to the letters of Paul for uncovering the mystery of "the church." Paul writes, for example, "So we, though many, are one body in Christ and individually parts of one another" (Romans 12:5). Later, Paul will write of Christ: "He is the head of the body, the church" (Colossians 1:18)." Surely Jesus Christ is the One for whom we long.

Jesus calls his followers to share in the life he came to bring in all its abundance. We are real people, with real needs and real challenges right now. We live for the fullness of life and experience the risen Christ in the reality and mystery of our daily lives. Often this occurs as we serve together in our parish community.

To be a member of a community that stands for some things and against others is part of what it means to belong to the church. Indeed to live by the faith of the church includes certain values and attitudes and excludes others. We depend on our bishops—our shepherds—for leadership and guidance as we live for the fullness of life in contemporary society.

Many examples of people blending reality and mystery in living for the fullness of life are given us by the saints. In the chart below, labeled with names of some saints, enter the names of whomever you wish to remember as you look back on your life of faith. Perhaps these people have been saintlike to you, models of discipleship, and you may want to thank them in prayer and in person for their support of your efforts to live the Christian life with your sisters and brothers in faith.

Saints Past and Present

Mary	Teresa of Avila	Peter
John		Mark
Mary Magdalene		Clare
Francis of Assisi		Catherine
Luke	Elizabeth Ann Seton	Paul

Living the faith of the church also involves sharing in a vision and hope of what your parish can be and deciding to become or remain an active parishioner. Think for a moment of what our newly baptized may be thinking during this afterglow of the triduum. Perhaps they are asking, "What power of water is this, that my life can be so dramatically changed? How is this water, poured in the liturgy of baptism, a vehicle for sharing in such abundant life?"

The power of the water is a power we trace to the Holy Spirit, who is with us too as we walk the path of new life that is ours—for a lifetime—in baptism. We are called to be full of faith and to join with our newly baptized as they deepen their lively faith. Who knows, support of just one of these newly baptized by you may become a turning point in that person's life.

- *How do you feel now about your parish? Is there something you would like to change; something you like just the way it is? What might you do?*

Accepting the Challenge

As you look back on your journey of faith, try to recall memories that go beyond words spoken over the years. Focus too on what leads you to be open to the Holy Spirit in your life. Recall your emotions, your joys, your tears. In other words look at the whole you rather than only what lies within your mind. Search out the presence of God deep within.

Our joy is not a naive good feeling by which we are able to avoid the hard issues of life: issues like accepting oneself; wounded relationships; strained communication between parents and children. We may also be puzzled over why a friend seems to undergo one terrible loss after another; or why a baby is born with a congenital birth defect; or being unable to leave angry words behind and hold a loved one.

The joy of discipleship is a convincing yes to life in all its struggles and difficulties—in all its abundance. It is more of a joyful attitude conceived in the heart. Rather than an escape, it is an acceptance of life's problems in a spirit pregnant with hope and trust, confident that the Holy Spirit is with you and your faith community.

Consider asking two or three people from your parish why they remain faithful to the church. Encourage them to go beyond the obvious reasons you would expect to hear. Then ask yourself what you think will cause you to remain true to the faith you profess. Perhaps the following will aid your reflection.

• *Name one challenge you had to face last week. What insight did you gain from this experience?*

Pray always for a spirit of openness in your heart. Seek an attitude of deep joy and longing for the fullness of life. As you conclude this chapter, consider again the words of Jesus from today's gospel: "I came so that they might have life and have it more abundantly" (John 10:10). Rejoice in the gift of new life that is yours!

Prayer for the Week

God the Holy Spirit,
   you probe the depths of my life.
You know me inside out
   and rest within every fiber of my being.
You fill me with the fire of faith
   and move me to live as a disciple of Jesus Christ,
      the risen Son of God
      the eternal Word
      One with you
      in everlasting communion with the Father.
Surround me always with your abiding presence.
Satisfy my longing
and move my parish to be a model of the life
for which we yearn: life in abundance. Amen.
                              —Gerard F. Baumbach

CHAPTER 12:
WAY OF LIFE, TRUTH OF LIFE

Fifth Sunday of Easter

Exploring Your Experience

Have you ever been in a situation in which you found yourself saying something like this: "I am going to..." or "I am not about to..." or "I am hoping that..."? The fifth Sunday of Easter focuses on a powerful foundation for shaping the way you might complete these statements—a sensitive and compelling awareness of Jesus the Christ: way of life, truth of life.

Discovering your way of life is part of your search, your journey. For a caller to a radio helpline, the distant voice of a talk show personality may represent the comfort of someone who cares. But it may also represent a false hope, a kind of long distance consolation without benefit of intimacy, trust or one-on-one communication. Sometimes people may confide in others—family, friends, coworkers, even radio and TV personalities—and come away frustrated because they sense they are no better off than when they began. The person listening to them may be happy to listen, but unwilling or unable to commit to finding a solution.

- *Can you recall a time when you were facing a serious problem and sought help from another? How did you feel?*
- *Can you recall a time when you experienced a "letdown"*

due to another's unwillingness to get involved? Why do you think it happened this way?

The easy answer to life's questions may be: "I know the way—Jesus." Indeed, a popular bumper sticker states, "If you are lost, I know the way." As we see in today's gospel, Jesus told his followers, "I am the way and the truth and the life." Yet for two thousand years, unraveling the meaning of this statement has not been a simple process. In fact, misunderstanding of Jesus as "the way" has led to disharmony and sometimes hostility among church bodies that claim the name *Christian.* Sadly, ethnic or racial tension may exist in some places; some people may question one another's loyalty to "truth"; still others may attempt to judge the worth or "quality" of people's lives.

The key question, then, regarding your life in Christ may not be the standard one, "Who is Jesus?" Rather, it may be, "Who is Jesus for me?" How do *you* answer this question?

Exploring the Scriptures

The readings for the fifth Sunday of Easter are:

- *Acts of the Apostles 6:1–7*
- *1 Peter 2:4–9*
- *John 14:1–12*

At one point in his public ministry, Jesus asked his disciples, "'But who do you say that I am?' Peter said to him in reply, 'You are the Messiah'" (Mark 8:29). For your own response, search your heart and focus on your response to Jesus' question.

- *How is Jesus your way?*
- *How is Jesus your truth?*
- *How is Jesus your life?*

Acts of the Apostles 6:1-7

The story of the growth of the early church is told, in part, in the Acts of the Apostles. This brief passage tells about the selection of seven disciples to serve two different groups of Jewish Christians in Jerusalem. The passage reveals disagreement about practical issues among the early Christians—in this case, balancing the equitable distribution of resources with prayer and ministry of the word.

Think about decision making in your parish, family, company, school or some other group. Focus on what, in your opinion, motivates people to decide what to do in making important decisions. The passage from Acts notes that the disciples were to choose those who were "filled with the Spirit and wisdom."

What kinds of things are considered in making decisions in the group you selected? What do *you* consider when you have to make an important decision?

1 Peter 2:4-9

Cornerstone/Jesus Christ/living stone—this reading gives you the opportunity to continue to explore more about the way you relate to the cornerstone of our faith, Jesus Christ. He is a living cornerstone, the way to life now, as well as the timeless life that resides in eternal truth.

The symbolism of the stone is not a creation of the author of 1 Peter. The author draws from Old Testament notions—Isaiah 28:16 and Psalm 118:22—to lay the claim that Jesus is the living stone from which the believer draws life. For persons of faith in Jesus, the stone called Christ is more than just another lifeless or immovable object, weighed down by its own mass. It is the source and foundation of life, linking us not only to Christ but to one another.

With such reflection we can see again that we are one in relationship with others as we are one in Christ, the one whom death could not conquer. We act on our belief in Christ by being open to the breath of the Holy Spirit in our lives.

Now consider how you are a living stone. Do you have a new insight into the way you relate to another person? Can you assist in resolving a friend's personal problem? Might you sense the need for healing in your family, marriage or other relationship? Whatever the situation, you are called to share the life that is yours as best you can. When you do this, you are being a living stone.

- *Close your eyes and relax your senses. Clear your head of thoughts and distractions. Before you open your eyes, try to decide on one specific thing you will do this week to support another person.*

John 14:1–12

Sometimes people feel terribly alone: the person who has just lost a job, the couple whose baby is seriously ill, the family suffering with a loved one with Alzheimer's disease. All need reassurance that the situation is somehow manageable, no matter how hopeless it may seem.

Jesus' reassuring words that begin this discourse to his disciples are a "calm down" message to them: "Do not let your hearts be troubled./You have faith in God; have faith also in me." The disciples are troubled by Jesus' pending separation from them. They don't want to be alone! Neither do we. Jesus urges his followers to maintain trust in him. One senses that Jesus is trying to help them, and us, put together pieces of a complex puzzle. To the quizzical Thomas, Jesus replies, "I am the way and the truth and the life."

Jesus tries to help his followers come to see not only who he is but also what they are called to become. Jesus gives each of us the same encouragement. In and through Jesus we find the way of life, the truth of life.

Jesus is the way—he is not just the one who shows the way to freedom, but is freedom itself. In Jesus we find salvation. Jesus is the truth—not only a great prophet telling the truth about God's love for people, but the living truth of who God is. Jesus is also the life—again, not some great preacher who only sets out rules and norms, but in him there is life itself. Jesus and his Father are one. Jesus is the way to the God of all truth, the source of all life.

As you pause to explore your relationship with Christ—formed within your local community of faith—remember that conversion is not some robotic response. Conversion takes a lifetime, as you come to live the hope of the risen Lord. It is a process that gives you pause, beckoning you to believe in Jesus day after day as your way, truth and life. What sweet reassurance this is for us. Our challenge is to trust in God, oneself and in the willingness of others to provide support and hope all life long.

- *Is there someone who needs your reassurance now? How might you respond?*
- *In this passage Jesus says that "whoever believes in me will do the works that I do,/and will do greater ones than these...." Imagine for a moment that the future of the world is in your hands. The only limitation you have is that you are not permitted to use words to achieve whatever goal you set for yourself. What gesture(s) would you use? Why?*

Renewing Your Life of Faith

Jesus' demonstration that he is way, truth and life can give new meaning to the way you choose to live. For example, gathering with others for worship can become more than maintaining a weekly practice that may have become routine. Gathering for the eucharistic liturgy just might help to develop an awareness of what it means to worship with others, and draw or give support from or to them for the week to come. The celebration of the sacrament of the Lord's body and blood may result in transforming us as we live as a united community called "the church." Deciding to join a particular parish may lead to becoming an active member of this local community of faith.

The eucharist is the one sacrament of initiation that we are called to celebrate over and over again. Through it, all assembled are united in faith, transformed by the body and blood of Christ. In the sacrificial meal of the eucharist we offer a sacrifice of praise to God. Catholics celebrate the gift of Jesus really present under the appearances of bread and wine, now become his body and blood.

The eucharist is our nourishment for broken lives, hopeful lives, shaken lives, trusting lives, saddened lives and joyful lives.

What is it you experience during the celebration of eucharist? What makes the mass—your parish's sacred pause in time—so central to the community's ongoing life as disciples of the risen Lord? In the eucharist the church offers thanks for God's blessings, the greatest of which is Jesus—the way, the truth and the life.

- *Is there a particular part of the liturgy that helps you to focus on Jesus as your way, truth and life? the blessings and wonder of God?*

When viewing television, listening to the radio, surfing the web or reading the newspaper this week, try to pick up signals of what people hold as their way, truth and life. This is really a way of getting at what they value. Afterward, think of what you value. Then complete these statements.

• *I expected others to....*
• *I was surprised that I value...because....*

The eucharist is nourishment for your life as a follower of Jesus Christ. No one, really, can duplicate how you decide to live or how you express what you value. Remember, you are not alone. You are able to shape your response to Jesus in the eucharist within the presence of and as part of your parish community. As St. Paul reminds us, "There are different kinds of spiritual gifts but the same Spirit; there are different forms of service but the same Lord; there are different workings but the same God who produces all of them in everyone" (1 Corinthians 12:4–6).

Accepting the Challenge

Do you ever get confused between what you may be told is *the* way to follow Jesus and the best way for you? One person's way may not be possible or beneficial for another. Indeed, people may find different ways of expressing in daily life their faith in Jesus Christ.

You can get confused if you try to imitate others and find yourself unable to accomplish what you set out to do. For example, a parishioner you know may have a great ability for working with young people or be just the right person for coordinating parish human service programs. You, on the other hand, may feel uncertain about participating in either of these ministries. Instead of talking yourself into trying to be like someone else, it might be more productive to explore your own gifts and abilities and how your parish might benefit from them.

You might conclude that your focus for living is to be only on Jesus. You may want to visualize such a simple approach with a straight line connecting yourself to Jesus. However, what if the perception of Jesus as way, truth and life was expressed through relationships with others as essential to what it means to live in Christ? Picture a series of circles of increasing size, one inside the next. Each ring is a set of relationships in your life, and at the very center is your own life formed by the life of Christ. In this view, the way you relate to others is shaped and enriched by your relationship with Christ. Way, truth and life begin to take on meanings perhaps never thought of before, as a believer begins to explore the impact of one's faith in Christ upon how one relates to others.

In this Easter season of celebrating Jesus as way of life and truth of life, ask yourself to probe even more. After all, if you claim Jesus as your way, how might you offer another person a glimpse of "the way" on your faith journey? If Jesus is your truth, who is it who has helped you to see this truth? If Jesus is your life, what lives of others have been examples to you of this teaching? In the end, know the presence of the saving One, who comes to you for you and through you for others.

Prayer for the Week

Lord Jesus,
    you come in simplicity as our way.
    Show us the way.
    You come in reassuring love as our truth.
    Be our truth through all time.
    You penetrate our lives with yours.
    Help us to know the wonder of your life in the
        midst of the wonders of the lives you
        entrust to us.
Praised be you, Lord Jesus Christ, the Son of God,
    Way of Life and Truth of Life
    now and forever. Amen.
                —Gerard F. Baumbach

CHAPTER 13:
HOLY SPIRIT, LOVING LORD

Sixth Sunday of Easter

Exploring Your Experience

"That's the spirit!" "Put some life into it!" "Give it all you've got!"

Who or what urges you to press onward when you are struggling? Who or what offers you a compelling sense of inner resourcefulness to move ahead? Or to step back and scan the horizon?

Many of us might identify someone who serves as a gentle reminder of the Holy Spirit alive in our hearts.

You may experience an urging of the Holy Spirit from deep within to gather with others for worship and to look at your own life, nourished by eucharist, as a source of hope, strength and life to others.

The Holy Spirit truly is our life source, opening our hearts and moving us to heal, to love and to care for one another. The living presence of God penetrates our lives, urging us to live as temples of the Spirit (cf. 1 Corinthians 6:19).

Exploring the dynamics of your inner striving and yearning and blooming spirituality may help you to discover what keeps you going: God, goals, family, friends, faith and so on. Your exploration is enriched by your experience of life, including some of life's peak moments: times of birth and death; injury and healing; despair and hope.

- *What people or events help you to know the presence of the Holy Spirit in your life? to testify to the presence and power of the Spirit among those you love especially?*

Exploring the Scriptures

The Holy Spirit may be characterized as moving among us so powerfully that any description is light years from being adequate. However, the Bible gives us one important source for coming to an understanding of the Holy Spirit. The church reminds us of the Spirit's movement among us, prompting our faithful response to God's call in our lives.

As you read the scriptures, seek a heightened awareness of the movement of the Holy Spirit in your life.

The readings for the sixth Sunday of Easter are:

- *Acts of the Apostles 8:5–8, 14–17*
- *1 Peter 3:15–18*
- *John 14:15–21*

Acts of the Apostles 8:5–8, 14–17

This reading is from that part of the Acts of the Apostles that describes how the gospel message about Jesus was preached through Judea and Samaria. It tells of the work of Philip and of his journey from Jerusalem to Samaria to preach the word of God. (See Acts 6:1–7.)

The passage demonstrates the link between the baptism of the Samaritans and the completion of their baptism through the laying on of hands by the apostles Peter and John. People in the town of Samaria responded to Philip's preaching, but their response could not be complete without the imposition of hands, a sign of the gift of the Holy Spirit in their lives.

This action of the imposition of hands reminds us even today of the coming of the Holy Spirit into our lives. Ponder briefly one or more of these prophetic witnesses to the presence of God in the life of the community that gave birth, in Jesus, to Christianity.

- The spirit of the LORD shall rest upon him. (Isaiah 11:2)
- The spirit of the Lord GOD is upon me,/because the LORD has anointed me. (Isaiah 61:1)
- I will give you a new heart and place a new spirit within you....(Ezekiel 36:26)
- Then afterward I will pour out/my spirit upon all mankind. (Joel 3:1)

- *As you rest in the presence of God, stretch your memory to the earliest promptings of the Holy Spirit in your life. Recall childhood or later memories, and the decisions you made to welcome God into your life. Know the ongoing presence of the One whom Jesus promised.*

1 Peter 3:15–18

In this reading we come across the phrase "life in the Spirit." Jesus, "brought to life in the Spirit," is our hope in suffering and our joy when we confront whatever might divert us from living as disciples of the Lord Jesus Christ. Sadly, some people may see such things as aiding a housebound neighbor or supporting world hunger relief as only distant challenges to living as witnesses to the One who suffered for all.

Peter urges followers of Christ to accept criticism "with gentleness and reverence." They are to remember that the source of their way of life is Jesus Christ, the risen Lord. As you reflect on this reading, continue to think of your life as the life of the Spirit and of how the virtue of hope helps you to live out your baptism, acting on behalf of people in need.

One phrase that could go unnoticed in this passage is this one: "...that he might lead you to God." Jesus suffers for all, is brought to new life and in so doing leads us to God...the God who calls and who comes, who leaves us not alone but together in life, faith, hope and love.

It is possible that we could overlook, perhaps unconsciously, our responsibility to help others know Christ. Think for a moment of who it is who helps lead you to God day by day, week after week, year after year. Is it only your own response to Christ? Might it also be persons who have influenced you all during your life?

Continue to be open to living in the Spirit so that you may "[s]anctify Christ as Lord in your hearts."

- *Try to identify an event, individual or community that leads you to God. Why do you think there is such an effect on you?*
- *Who, for you, is a symbol of the hope that Christians believe in? Why?*

John 14:15–21

This passage begins Jesus' last address to his disciples before his death. You may notice that the first and last verses of the passage include Jesus' use of the word *love*. He seems intent on assuring his followers of his presence with them always. As you read the passage, think about someone you love and how you can show your love for him or her today.

In John's gospel, we come across a word found in none of the other gospels: *Paraclete*. The Paraclete is the Holy Spirit, but the meaning of *Paraclete* may be clarified by such words as *helper, counselor, comforter* or *advocate*. One might also apply these terms to Jesus, who demonstrated all these roles in his public ministry.

Jesus promised to send the Holy Spirit to help his followers after he would no longer be with them. The promised Holy Spirit came to and strengthened the disciples on Pentecost Sunday. We are called to trust in this unseen Spirit who resides within the believer. The root of this trust is the love between Jesus and the believer.

In an age as technologically oriented as ours, such talk of spiritual realities may indeed appear odd, perhaps even a contradiction. Spiritual matters do not lend themselves to computerlike analysis, and so we may be inclined to avoid or dismiss them. Discussion of our lives in relationship with Jesus Christ is full of possibilities. These possibilities focus on the reality of new life born of the death and resurrection of Jesus and nourished by the Holy Spirit, truly present in the lives of the disciples after the resurrection and in our lives two millennia later.

Another theme from today's gospel is that of the love of Jesus for his disciples. Within John's gospel, this account appears soon after Jesus had washed the feet of his disciples at the Passover meal. This washing was a gesture of love, and came just before Jesus told his followers: "I give you a new commandment: love one another. As I have loved you, so you also should love one another. This is how all will know that you are my disciples, if you have love for one another" (13:34–35).

Jesus asks his followers to obey the commands he gives them as a sign of his love for them.

We are challenged to keep the commandments first given to Moses centuries before Jesus was born. Indeed, Jesus had told his followers that he had come to fulfill the law and not to abolish it. The new commandment of Jesus does not replace the commandments given to Moses. Rather, it is an important moral foundation for living, for keeping the commandments and for loving as Jesus had loved.

- *Helper, counselor, comforter, advocate: Are any of these words helpful in clarifying the movement of the Holy Spirit in your life? If so, how?*
- *To help you not judge others hastily, what might you do?*

Renewing Your Life of Faith

One help for exploring the role of the Holy Spirit in your life may be to recover, as Paul the apostle did, the Old Testament notion of the life-giving Spirit. Paul's New Testament writings have a variety of references to the Holy Spirit as the life-giving and life-sustaining force in the world. For example, Paul points out that "Such confidence we have through Christ toward God....[God] has indeed qualified us as ministers of a new covenant, not of letter but of spirit; for the letter brings death, but the Spirit gives life" (2 Corinthians 3:4–6).

Focusing on the Holy Spirit as life-giving and as the source of life may lead you to explore with new eyes the treasure of your relationship in Christ.

Recall your confirmation. Were you a young child? An adolescent? A young or older adult? Confirmation—being sealed with the gift of the life-giving Spirit—celebrates the outpouring of the gift of the Holy Spirit in one's life. Sealed with the Holy Spirit by means of the anointing with sacred chrism, you can decide daily to live "life in the Spirit." Like baptism, confirmation may never be repeated; the gift of the Holy Spirit is both life-giving and a gift for life, in union with the risen Christ. Recall these words of Paul to the Romans: "[T]he love of God has been poured out into our hearts through the Holy Spirit that has been given to us" (5:5).

Confirmation is linked to baptism and to eucharist, the other sacraments of initiation. The powerful activity of the Holy Spirit moves through and beyond baptism and confirmation. It is especially expressed in the eucharist and in the community of gathered believers. Our experience of the mass becomes for us an important source for uncovering together the power and meaning of the mystery of God present in our parish, now and always.

In the thanksgiving of eucharist, we enter into Christ's saving death and resurrection. The sacrifice that Jesus offered on the cross is made real and present at mass; Jesus, fully human and fully divine, is really present in the eucharist under the appearances of bread and wine. We participate in this memorial today, transformed into a people with a life-giving mission that originates with Christ.

From the weekly eucharistic celebration emerges a bridge between liturgy and life, resulting in an awareness of the need to share the graced life with others. The Holy Spirit not only moves us to come together for worship, but also to go from worship to serve others.

The Spirit calls us to be open to others with compassion and trust, justice and charity. Our nourishment for such living is from the eucharist, nourishing us and urging us to handle with care the gift of new life given in Christ. By the way we live, we become even more visibly the body of Christ in the unity of the Holy Spirit.

• *Pause now to reflect on the Holy Spirit, who motivates you to worship and to adhere to the faith you profess. The Holy Spirit not only beckons you to gather with others for eucharist, but also to act in Jesus' name.*

Renewing Faith: The Feast of the Ascension

Near the end of the Easter season is the feast of the Ascension. On this day we recall Jesus' return to the Father following his resurrection. Three scripture readings are proclaimed.

The first is from the beginning of the Acts of the Apostles (1:1–11). The passage includes this scriptural account of Jesus' ascension: "[H]e was lifted up, and a cloud took him from their sight."

The second reading is from Paul's letter to the Ephesians (1:17–23). Paul calls the God of Jesus "the Father of glory" and asserts his belief in Christ as "head over all things to the church,/which is his body,/the fullness of the one who fills all things in every way."

The last reading is from the final verses of the gospel according to Matthew (28:16–20). In this gospel ending, the risen Jesus commissions the eleven disciples to go and baptize others "in the name of the Father, and of the Son, and of the Holy Spirit." Jesus assures his followers that he would be with them always.

• *During the next week, select one of these readings for your reflection. Consider Jesus' presence in the circumstances of your life during this Easter season.*

Accepting the Challenge

Jesus' call to love is not just a plea to those who were present with him at the Passover meal before his death on the cross. It is a call to all people of good will, urging them not simply to love one another, but to love as Jesus had first loved them. This is a "spirit-love," a love whose source is God and whose expression is human love. Such love calls us to be "Christ" not only to one another in our parish, but to all others as well. What a challenge!

Perhaps you sense that movement toward love sometimes is met by resistance and suspicion. For some people, for example, unless an issue is in the newspapers, it does not exist at all. The evening news—with occasional spot reports on unsettling world conditions, mushrooming epidemics, latent racist attitudes, violence of various kinds and so on—provides only a momentary glimpse of a lack of love that may not affect directly the viewer or reader.

These and other social issues sometimes may remain hidden from people's consciousness, even while other love-denying realities occur on a more personal level: families whose members are not on speaking terms, neighborhoods where peace warrants exist between homeowners, employer-employee relations saddled with distrust and malice.

Indeed, challenges to the pursuit of justice can confront us at work, at home, at school, anywhere. Regardless of their source, or even misplaced assertions that they are "political" or have little to do with "family spiritual growth," such love-denying realities must be blotted out.

Obviously, people's response to Jesus' call to people to love, to build the reign of God, has far to go. Yet as Christians we *do* believe that we *can* live as Jesus' disciples, and together accept his call and act on his mission.

• *One question worth considering now is, How might your sharing in the eucharist move you to continue to live justly? to chip away at antilove values and attitudes of which you are aware?*

As you explore what it is that brings you together with others in the eucharist, you may discover more about the presence of the Holy Spirit in your life. Perhaps this journey within can be another important fruit of all you do in gathering with others for eucharist and as a disciple of the risen One, Jesus Christ.

Prayer for the Week

Come, Holy Spirit
   be with me
   dwell within me
   comfort me
   envelop me with the gift of your love
   rest within my soul
   and burn within me the fire of faith
   in your everlasting love.
Empower me to be one with others in my parish
   that we may love one another as our Lord Jesus Christ
   has first loved us
   that we may fulfill others' needs
   and not abolish them
   and that our every parish action, program and event
   may be a sign of your presence with us always
   for your honor and glory. Amen.
—Gerard F. Baumbach

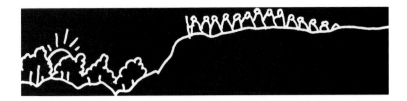

CHAPTER 14:
FAITH LIVED, MISSION SHARED

Seventh Sunday of Easter

Exploring Your Experience

Conversion to a Christian way of life usually takes time. That is why the word *journey* has been used in this book. Journeys take time. Often, they take commitment, risk, pain, challenge and change.

After these weeks of reflection during Lent and Easter, you may feel that you are discovering anew what it is to live a life centered in the Holy Spirit every day.

Our mission for a life of faith originates with Jesus Christ, Son of God and Savior of the world. Our mission develops over a lifetime, and no one can live your faith or believe for you. How you live your faith is all part of coming to grips with your mission for a life of faith.

In finding Jesus, who came to give life to the full, we can begin to seek him even more. Fully divine and fully human, Jesus experienced the ups and downs of life as did others of his time—in all things but sin.

If we look to Luke 4:18–19, we get a glimpse of Jesus' mission. Jesus says in the temple: "The Spirit of the Lord is upon me,/ because he has anointed me to bring glad tidings to the poor./He has sent me to proclaim liberty to captives/and recovery of sight to the blind, to let the oppressed go free,/and to proclaim a year acceptable to the Lord."

Beneath this mission, and supporting it, was a strong connection to his Father in prayer. When he prayed, Jesus called God *Abba,* the Aramaic word for father. The letter to the Hebrews states, "In the days when he was in the flesh, he offered prayers and supplications with loud cries and tears to the one who was able to save him from death, and he was heard because of his reverence" (5:7).

For us today, prayer and personal reflection may result in hearing pleas for assistance from individuals, human service or other care-giving organizations or other groups. As you continue with this chapter, try to think about your mission as you continue your journey of faith.

- *When you hear someone say, "You have a mission!", what do you think of first? Why is that?*
- *As you continue your journey, might you need to consider changing the way you live your faith commitment?*

Exploring the Scriptures

One of the characteristics of Jesus' life was the consolation he found in prayer. The scripture readings for this Sunday focus in part on the prayer of Jesus and the early disciples of the church. When you read these passages, consider the linkages between prayer and our mission for a life of faith.

The readings for the seventh Sunday of Easter are:

- *Acts of the Apostles 1:12–14*
- *1 Peter 4:13–16*
- *John 17:1–11a*

Acts of the Apostles 1:12–14

This passage begins just after Jesus was taken from the sight of his disciples (recall the account of the Ascension from chapter 13). Perhaps out of anticipation of Jesus' return, the disciples go back to Jerusalem. The center of the early church was Jerusalem. This historic and rebuilt city was no stranger to religious groups, and so the disciples elect to return and stay together there. As you read the passage, try to identify one or more important journeys of your own.

As the passage points out, the disciples occupied themselves with prayer. Prayer was an important part of the disciples' discernment of their mission in following Jesus' way. We may wonder what went through their minds as they prayed together. The mysterious happenings of the previous days may have left them awe-filled yet confused. And now Jesus bids them farewell and vanishes from their sight!

When we think that Jesus is absent from our life, that may be just the right time to turn to prayer. Some people may think of prayer as no more than asking God for "things to turn out OK." Prayer is much more than that. Through prayer we may pause and discover in the quiet of our heart the presence of the Holy Spirit. Such a discovery may be a source of strength to rebuild an uncertain relationship, to speak up on behalf of human dignity, to move ahead to an unexpected future or to maintain the status quo with renewed hope. Prayer is an important help as we live our mission for a life of faith.

• *When do you pray? Why do you pray?*

1 Peter 4:13–16

The theme for this reading is a return to a theme discussed elsewhere in this book—that of suffering. Think briefly of two or three recent events that remind you of people's struggles in life. Ask yourself if any good could possibly result from the suffering or struggles.

Peter addresses his comments to Christians who are Gentiles in Asia Minor. He urges them to maintain their identity as Christians in the face of unkindness from those neighbors who are not part of their religious body.

A Christian bears suffering for the name of Christ, and the ultimate effect of such suffering is life forever with the risen Christ. The reading points out that the Holy Spirit is with those who suffer. Jesus' suffering and death on the cross are particularly sacred yet challenging dimensions of what it means to live as a Christian. Ongoing spiritual direction may help us discover levels of meaning of these and other aspects of Christian belief. It may also help us to discern the promptings of the Spirit in our lives.

There are certain sufferings of the heart, characterized by a willingness to accept the consequences of a decision, however difficult, for what we believe must be done. In fact, the decision may be one over which we have no control; the situation may involve physical torment as well. For example, the great tragedy of the Holocaust includes stories of heroism and risk on the part of a people determined to survive despite incredible odds against them.

- *Is there someone you know who is suffering now? What could you do to express your care for that person?*
- *How might your faith in Christ help you to deal with suffering you may be experiencing now?*

John 17:1–11a

The gospel reading is Jesus' great prayer before he was arrested and sentenced to death. His prayer reveals a touching intimacy with his Father. As you read the passage, you may want to think about your own experience of prayer, its impact on your life of faith and on your relationship with God.

The prayer that Jesus utters in this passage is delivered with intensity. He is about to undergo arrest, suffering and death. He turns to his Father in prayer and in so doing recalls his mission on earth: "I glorified you on earth/by accomplishing the work that you gave me to do." Jesus also reflects on the faithfulness of his disciples, noting their acceptance of his own ministry and message.

Jesus' work was not limited to doing helpful things for people; in healing and comforting others, Jesus was revealing God to them. In doing this, he helped people begin to discover and even taste the life of God that is described by the word *eternal*. When Jesus prayed, "I revealed your name...," he may have really been acknowledging who he *was* and *is* in revealing and sharing with others the very life of God.

- *Imagine yourself alongside the first followers of Jesus. You hear him say the words of this passage. Is there a part of the passage that puzzles you? What is it? What would you ask Jesus to help you understand better?*
- *What might enable you to carry on the work of Jesus in the ordinary experiences of life each day?*

Renewing Your Life of Faith

Each gathering for eucharist is an opportunity to pray with others in thanksgiving to God for the gift of Jesus really present, and to assert with other believers the willingness of the local parish to put into practice what it has professed in faith. In this way, our parish may be able to clarify its own mission as a Christian community enlivened by the Holy Spirit.

What is the relation between the Spirit and the eucharist? Four aspects of the eucharist may help us to see the relation of the Holy Spirit with the eucharist and the linkage between our faith and the way we live it. The four aspects, rooted in the church's celebration of the liturgy, are eucharist as meal, as thanksgiving, as real presence of Christ and as sacrifice.

We come to the table of the Lord, that altar of life around which we gather for the sacred meal. In this banquet we gather in praise of God, who gives us life, nourishment and the hope of future glory. The sacred food of the eucharist is broken and shared among our gathered assembly during the communion rite of the mass. We are nourished and go forth to live as disciples of the Lord and yearn to return to the table again.

The root meaning of the word *eucharist* is "thanksgiving." We offer in thanks to the Father the One who gave himself for us. The Spirit moves a Christian, like you, to thank God for the gift of Jesus in the eucharist. Indeed, the whole eucharistic prayer is an expression of thanksgiving to God. What are you thankful for? How else do you offer thanks in your life?

The real presence of Christ has been, perhaps, one of the most difficult aspects of faith for people to believe in. How, after all, can the bread and wine be Jesus? The church teaches that the bread and wine really become the body and blood of Christ. What appears to be bread and wine is no longer bread and wine, but Christ himself, whom we receive in communion.

Sharing in the eucharist is not just for those who do so, but also has as its goal the unity of the church brought about by the Holy Spirit. For a Christian, another question may be how one is actually present to and united with others. We may ponder quietly now how we can be happy and at peace with others and how we can see Christ in them. How can we be a sign of Christ's presence to others?

Finally, the eucharist is a sacrifice. The sacrifice of Christ on the cross is really present in our celebration. The ultimate sacrifice is Jesus' complete and total giving of himself for all humanity. Through his passion, death, resurrection and ascension—the paschal mystery—Jesus gains and sustains for us life with God, not for one day, one year or one decade, but forever.

The eucharist is the sacrifice of the cross in which all of us assembled participate—an offering of Christ and the entire church to the Father. We enter into this sacred memorial and look to God for the strength to serve others in the name of Jesus. The Holy Spirit calls us to participate in the sacrifice and to commit ourselves to living as best we can in the Spirit of Christ.

- *What situations from your life remind you of your ongoing need for the eucharist?*
- *Fasting remains one important means of sacrifice for many Christians. Probe Isaiah 58:6-7 for another challenging meaning of fasting. Does this passage open new ways for you to say yes to the presence of the risen Christ in your life?*

Renewing Faith at Pentecost

The last day of the Easter season is Pentecost Sunday. On this day the church celebrates the coming of the Holy Spirit on the disciples of Christ. Reflect now on the Spirit in your life in light of the readings from Pentecost Sunday and your understanding of your mission for a life of faith.

The first reading, from the Acts of the Apostles (2:1-11), is the account of the coming of the Holy Spirit on Jesus' disciples. They were gathered together in one place "and they were all filled with the Holy Spirit" (2:4). The Spirit prompted the disciples to speak of the wonders of God. Two thousand years later, we believe with great fervor in the nearness and promptings of the Holy Spirit in our lives, too.

The second reading, from Paul's first letter to the Corinthians (12:3b-7, 12-13), includes Paul's classic statement on the many members of the body being one in Christ. We are baptized into one body. However, Paul also notes that "To each individual the manifestation of the Spirit/is given for some benefit." This is a point that may easily be forgotten. The Spirit is given to advance the growth of the whole church community; all benefit as each one's gift is given and shared.

The gospel reading for Pentecost Sunday is from the gospel of John (20:19–23). It also was proclaimed as part of the gospel for the second Sunday of Easter. In this gospel, the risen Christ tells his followers: "As the Father has sent me, so I send you./...Receive the Holy Spirit."

- *Do you believe that you are "sent by God" for any particular mission or purpose? What might you do tomorrow to remind yourself of the Holy Spirit present in your life?*
- *What decision might you make that could affect the good of all?*

Accepting the Challenge

Life for a Christian is not some rainbow type of existence characterized by peak moments of wonder, awe and joy. Conversion to Christ may be an ongoing journey through paths of doubt as well as faith, loss as well as hope, sadness as well as joy. It also looks to a vibrant prayer life nourished by the sacraments of the church. It is, in a word, life lived in the power and the presence of the indwelling Holy Spirit.

We are called to carry out our mission and live out the faith believed and celebrated in an outreach to others called ministry. The call to serve is a reminder of Jesus' plea to his disciples to "love one another. As I have loved you, so you also should love one another" (John 13:34). We can live this mission by making sense of how our sharing in the eucharist may affect our daily experiences with others.

There are many ways to help in parish ministry. Parish life may include service in such diverse areas as catechesis, worship, Christian initiation sponsor, justice and peace work, social services, physical plant upkeep, communications and so on.

There is no exact solution to the ways you may continue or the way you may begin to participate in the life of your parish. Whatever you do, remember that ministry does not have to be some eye-popping, soap box performance. It can be whatever you decide to make it, as you choose the best way to live out life in Christ along with others in your parish. Indeed, by looking at yourself as in a mirror, you may see where some answers for your questions about service lie: in yourself.

- *Is the Holy Spirit moving you to act in a way you don't understand clearly? to act differently at home or at work? to explore a new ministry in your parish?*

Endnote

One role we have as we live the Christian life is that of being a link, or bridge builder, between people. Perhaps you have had the opportunity to bring disagreeing people together, if not to reconcile then at least to talk. We might speculate that such beginning steps toward healing are actually an important first step to reducing world tensions. Perhaps a modern day prophet would challenge people and nations to race to embrace rather than to distrust and potentially destroy.

Remember your constant journey to the eucharist. Your journey began with your baptism. Through the waters of new life, you have come again and again to the table of the Lord, the table of hope and of life eternal. It is here we meet Christ the Lord, enveloping us with eternal love and goodness.

Continue to reflect, to face challenges in your decision making, to live each day, each moment with vigor and enthusiasm for the faith you profess. Know that your parish is with you, that the eyes, ears, hands, feet and hearts of good and holy people of faith are with you in prayer, in spirit, in trust, in life, in Christ—in all things. Remain part of a eucharistic people, a lively discipleship people in a society that needs your witness and your wisdom.

Lent-Easter time now draws to a close at Pentecost. So, what can your time beyond Pentecost become?

Time is no more than our concrete measure of the divine gift of life, experience and love of the Creator in our midst. So, see beyond the days of a calendar, the digital readout of a watch, the hands of a clock, the sands of an hourglass. Listen to more than the uniform measure of a ticking timepiece; continue to listen to the source of new life—life in Christ—that moves before, after, above, below, through and in time.

Know forever the timeless wonder and endless love of God. Enter into the worship of the church and, with the whole church, know the limitless love of God.

May your walk in the Christian life be ever fresh, ever faithful, ever joyful! Rejoice and be one with the God who saves and with your beloved sisters and brothers in faith, the church. Build bridges of mercy, justice and hope as you grow in the life of faith that radiantly shines forth all life long. May you assert with the whole church: Praised be Jesus Christ, now and forever!

Prayer for the Week

Gracious God,
    you stay with me
    you keep me whole
    you give me the endurance
    to stay the course
    each day of my life.
May I rest always in your Spirit, Lord,

and proclaim through my words and actions
the wonder of your name, the glory of your Son,
and the eternal hope of life forever with you.
My Lord and my God,
guide me to make my parish strong,
to be your hands to all who cry for help,
to offer the endless gift of your love to all.
Thank you, Lord, and praise you forever. Amen.

—Gerard F. Baumbach